Sewing
pretty little things

HOW TO MAKE SMALL BAGS AND
CLUTCHES FROM FABRIC REMNANTS

Design Originals

an Imprint of Fox Chapel Publishing
www.d-originals.com

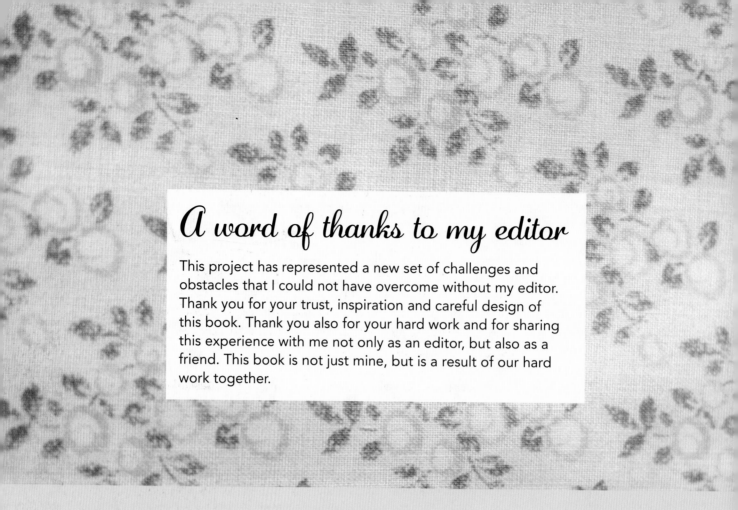

A word of thanks to my editor

This project has represented a new set of challenges and obstacles that I could not have overcome without my editor. Thank you for your trust, inspiration and careful design of this book. Thank you also for your hard work and for sharing this experience with me not only as an editor, but also as a friend. This book is not just mine, but is a result of our hard work together.

Handmade Gifts: 38 Projects of Remnants (手作小確幸。禮物組！:美布無剩超完美提案！)
by Cherie Lee
Copyright © 2011 by SYSTEX CORPORATION
All rights reserved.
English translation copyright © New Design Originals Corporation, an imprint of Fox Chapel Publishing, 2014
Published by arrangement with SYSTEX CORPORATION through LEE's Literary Agency, Taiwan

Credits for the English Edition
Publisher: Carole Giagnocavo
Acquisition Editor: Peg Couch
Editor: Colleen Dorsey
Designer: Ashley Millhouse

ISBN 978-1-57421-611-0

Sewing Pretty Little Things is a revised and abridged translation of the original Chinese book. This version published by New Design Originals, an imprint of Fox Chapel Publishing Company, Inc., East Petersburg, PA.

Library of Congress Cataloging-in-Publication Data

Lee, Cherie.
 [Shou zuo xiao que xing, li wu zu. English]
 Sewing pretty little things / Cherie Lee.
     pages cm
 Includes index.
 Summary: "Presents step-by-step instructions on using small fabric remnants to create a variety of bags and clutches. Includes sixteen diverse projects like backpacks, evening bags, coin purses, and lunch bags, and a detailed techniques section of useful skills to apply to the projects."-- Provided by publisher.
 ISBN 978-1-57421-611-0 (pbk.)
 1. Textile crafts. 2. Sewing. I. Title.
 TT699.L4413 2013
 646'.3--dc23
           2013025472

Printed in China
First printing

About the Author

Cherie Lee has a long history of sewing and designing stunning handmade items in her native Taiwan. In 2006, Cherie established her own handmade brand, Love · Catmint, and began attending many creative design events and festivals, which she continues to participate in as both guest and presenter today. In 2008, Cherie began to focus her handmade projects on cozy accessories inspired by soft fabrics. Since starting her sewing journey, Cherie has been featured in the news and in several magazines, and has published two sewing books on indoor shoes. In 2012, she established Catmint Studio, where she spends her days working on her next batch of impressive projects. Through her brand Love · Catmint, Cherie shares the comfort and happiness of soft handmade goods with her customers, friends, and family.
www.lovecatmint.com

"I love to play around with small bits of fabric,
I love the bliss of handmade projects, and,
most of all, I love the satisfaction that you feel
when you look upon your finished project."

Publisher's Note

How many purses does a woman need? This question doesn't have a right or wrong answer, but it does have a common answer: more!

Sewing Pretty Little Things features sixteen bags and clutches to accompany any outfit and match any style. Sometimes a purse or bag provides that final touch to an outfit, that last element that ties everything together… but it's expensive to buy purse after purse to achieve the perfect look. That's the genius of *Sewing Pretty Little Things*: by making accessories from your own leftover fabrics, remnants on sale at the store, or even repurposed vintage fabrics, you can save money and create a unique new bag that matches your style and needs. Whether you need a handy makeup bag, a convenient drawstring tote, or a soft floral clutch, you'll be able to use the designs in this book with the fabrics you love to create the perfect pretty little thing.

Be sure to look for the companion volume to *Sewing Pretty Little Things*, coming up in late 2014, which will feature a variety of accessories from hats, slippers, and coin purses to camera cases, card folios, and wallets, all made from fabric remnants.

Taiwanese author Cherie Lee joins the rapidly growing collection of talented craft authors from around the world selected for inclusion in the Design Originals line. Known for its innovative topics and highly regarded authors, Design Originals will continue to bring the best selections of foreign and American craft books to North American readers. We love these books, and we hope you will, too. Enjoy!

Carole

Carole Giagnocavo
Publisher
carole@d-originals.com

Editor's Note

Planning this project has been both a wonderful, enjoyable experience as well as a challenging and difficult journey. There are those inevitable times when you are painstakingly trying to come up with an idea, only to find yourself continuously hitting a brick wall; but such times are counteracted when you find inspiration for a great idea that makes you so excited that you could jump up and dance. I have been lucky enough to share these delights and hardships during this project with the book's author, Cherie Lee.

After Cherie finished her 2010 work on handmade indoor shoes, she wanted to strike again while the iron was hot, so she immediately set out to start on a new handmade project. Cherie and I began brainstorming until, after hours of throwing ideas back and forth, we came up with the idea of handmade gifts using fabric remnants.

The sixteen projects in this book appeal to a variety of different interests and needs. The author's key motive for this book is to reach out to a more diverse audience with the best yet of her cloth-work books. In creating this varied set of gifts, the most important issue that was resolved is one of the most common problems constantly presenting itself to handmade products: what do you do with your leftover scraps of material? Those last fragments of cloth left over after you have finished your other projects are perfect for the bags and accessories in this book.

I hope that you will find that each of these projects can help to serve as sincere and meaningful gifts for yourself or for those you love.

Table of Contents

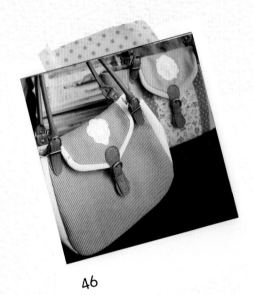

46

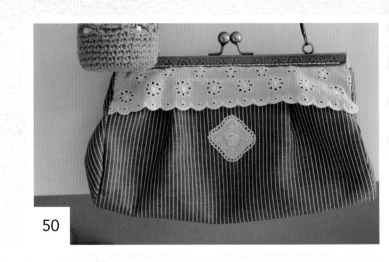

50

Bags

70

75

82

53

65

Clutches and Accessories

101

87

97

Introduction

One afternoon, my editor and I began discussing our thoughts for a new book, and as we chatted and bounced ideas back and forth, we finally came up with a plan.

This book of gifts has many purposes. I find that it is often difficult to express your emotions to the people closest to you; however, a gift can help deliver your most earnest wishes directly into the hands of those you love. This is truly the origin of the gift of giving, which is one of the underlying themes of this book.

We often tend to take care of others while neglecting our own wants and needs. However, loving oneself is also very important, and it is only by being good and truthful to ourselves that we may truly be loved by the people around us. I challenge you to first give the gift of happiness to yourself in order to allow your own heart to fill with contentment and joy. That means don't be afraid to make a bag or accessory for yourself!

I am constantly reminded of how fortunate I am. To be able to come up with creative ideas and spend time working on these handmade bags with friends is a blessing. To have the opportunity to make this book and share it with everyone is lucky. I am grateful also for the support that I have received from the growing number of people following my projects online. When I am happy, I look forward to making these handmade crafts, and when I am unhappy, I can turn to these projects to take my mind off of my worries. To be blessed is to be able to share your interests with others. This feeling of self-happiness is crucial in life, and I hope that I can always share this feeling.

Cherie Lee

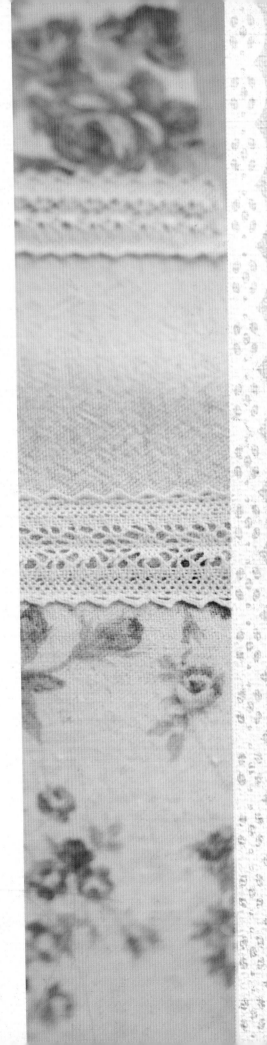

- Working Girl's Shoulder Bag
- Evening Bag
- Drawstring Bucket Purse
- Weekend Bag
- Casual Day Trip Purse
- Lunch Bag
- Everything Bag
- Travel Purse
- Vintage Gold Clasped Purse
- Backpack

Every day we sit at our desks, hard at work, but over time, long days start to take their toll. We look forward to when the clock hits 5, so we can run home and get back to our handmade projects—crawl into our cozy nooks, fool around with the cat, play with fabric, and reach the most relaxing and soothing part of the day. Life is meant to be enjoyed and full of love and inspiration, so give your hardworking self a special gift by making one of these handy bags, or give a bag as a gift to a friend or loved one. From bags for work, to bags for travel, to cute purses for a night out, these projects will delight you every day.

Working Girl's
Shoulder Bag

Instructions p. 46

Working Girl's Shoulder Bag

Making your own bag, aside from having the freedom to choose your own pattern, dimensions, and style, also means that you decide the size, placement, and number of pockets and compartments according to your needs. Take your own handmade bag into the office with you and share your creativity and satisfaction with those around you!

Evening Bag

Instructions p. 50

Evening Bag

This gold-clasped bag easily holds all of your essentials like your wallet and phone. The delicate, fashionable chain means this bag is ready for any dinner party or banquet!

Drawstring Bucket Purse

Instructions p. 53

Drawstring Bucket Purse

Playing hooky or just taking a few days off of school—or, for most of us, work!—is one of the best feelings in the world. Whether you go on a trip with friends, hang out at a local coffee shop, or visit a favorite bookstore, toss your essentials in this purse and make the most of your break!

Weekend Bag

This case has separate sections so that you can organize your necessaries to suit. You won't have to worry about a messy suitcase full of wrinkled clothes or jumbled items, and you will know exactly where to find what you need!

Make the other items pictured in this set in the sequel to this book, coming soon!

Weekend Bag

Instructions p. 55

Casual Day Trip Purse

A purse that you can take with you everywhere you go can truly be one of the best companions. One of the highlights of this purse is the adjustable strap, so you can fit it to the most comfortable length for you. With this purse over your shoulder, you will be ready to go anywhere!

Casual Day Trip Purse

Instructions p. 59

Make the other items pictured in this set in the
sequel to this book, coming soon!

Lunch Bag

Instructions p. 62

Lunch Bag

Do you remember being a kid at school and being jealous of your friends' cool lunch boxes? How about those days when your mom would pack you a special lunch that would brighten your entire day? Now you have the chance to make your own "cool" lunch bag and pack it with whatever food you like to eat. Whether you are a master chef or just a creative soul, your own homemade food always tastes the best and leaves you feeling good, as will carrying it in your own homemade bag.

Everything Bag

Instructions p. 65

Everything Bag

There are always plenty of little things that we like to keep in our purses. If your purse is big enough, with plenty of pockets, you can even keep it neat and tidy! However, there is always that tricky dilemma when you want to switch bags but don't want to forget any of your important items in the process.

With this bag, no matter where you are going or how often you want to switch bags, you can simply unclip the interior of the bag, take it out, and clip it into the bag of your choice! Now when you see a movie with friends on the weekend, hit the mall to shop, or go out for a meal, you can mix and match your bags without needing to worry.

Travel Purse

Are you having trouble finding a purse to use while traveling that is practical but still looks good? Do you need little front pockets for easy access to certain items? How about inside pockets for better organization, or a secure zipper pocket to keep your important belongings secure? Customize your own purse to fit your travel needs!

Travel Purse

Instructions p. 70

Vintage Gold
Clasped Purse

Instructions p. 75

Vintage Gold Clasped Purse

When you want to relax and treat yourself to a day out, bring this vintage-inspired purse with you! Take a stroll through the park, sit down at your favorite coffee shop, or meet a friend for a drink. This purse will make you feel good wherever you go and adds some old-fashioned flair to your look.

Backpack

Instructions p. 77

Backpack

Putting on this backpack will really take you back to the days of being a student. Right away you will feel the butterflies and excitement of getting ready for your first day of school. Even if it is only for a few hours, it's good to be a student again.

Part 2: Clutches and Accessories

Sometimes the smallest items are the loveliest—or the most useful! No matter if you are traveling near or far, the little projects featured here will serve your purposes and show off your style at the same time. Whether you need to carry coins for the bus or the meter, want to jot down your thoughts and notes in a covered notebook, or absolutely must have the perfect clutch to wear with your new outfit, you'll find the perfect pretty little thing here.

Compartment Clutch
_____

Instructions p. 82

Compartment Clutch

Sometimes you just want to carry your essentials. This small compartment clutch has been created to serve just such a purpose. There is a separate zipper pocket in the middle where you can safely store cash or credit cards. You can see in the pattern how to add a leather strap to the clutch so that you can keep this bag safely wrapped around your wrist at all times. Later, you can conveniently remove the strap and tuck the clutch into any purse or bag.

Chic Coin Purse

Do you ever find that when you go to the store, you are bombarded with long lines and floods of people hurrying to get what they need, so when you reach the cashier, you immediately pay with bills so that you aren't holding people up? After a while, your change piles up, filling first your coin purse and then your piggy bank to the brim. But if you find the right size coin purse, you can take it with you on all of your small errands, save those bills, and start spending that change!

Classy Clutch

Instructions p. 90

Classy Clutch

Small bags are great to just grab with one hand and take on the go. This bag can also be used as a makeup bag, so you can fill it with whatever accessories or belongings you want to have on hand while you're out and about.

Travel Notebook

Instructions p. 93

Travel Notebook

When preparing to embark on a new adventure, it is hard not to think of the many wonders awaiting you. Whether traveling to far off lands or nearby towns, you will discover many new people, places, and customs, so it is essential to find just the right notebook to bring with you and help you record all of your memories and experiences.

Gold Clasped Makeup Bag

How to Make p.97

Gold Clasped Makeup Bag

Girls always somehow have an abundance of small accessories that we like to carry with us wherever we go. It is therefore necessary to have a bag that can hold all of these items while still being handy and cute. This is a stylish cotton makeup bag that will be exactly what you need.

Handy Wristlet

Instructions p. 101

Handy Wristlet

With three inner compartments, this wristlet is as convenient as can be. It can carry your cell phone, money, cards, and keys, along with a few other small things such as lipstick or lotion. Your errands will become a simple and stress-free affair!

Instructions

Working Girl's Shoulder Bag

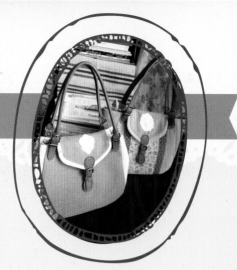

The finished shoulder bag measures 11⅞" x 9⅞" x 5⅞" (30 x 25 x 15cm).

MATERIALS:

- ⅓ yd. (⅓m) of medium-weight fabric for main bag
- ¼ yd. (¼m) of medium-weight complementing fabric for contrasting bag sections
- ⅔ yd. (⅔m) of lightweight fabric for lining
- ½ yd. (½ yd.) of lightweight complementing fabric for inside pockets
- 1¼ yds. (1¼m) of 44" (112cm) wide or 2¼ yd (2¼m) of 22" (56cm) wide heavyweight interfacing
- 8" (20.5cm) zipper
- 6⅝" x 4½" (17 x 11.5cm) piece of plastic board
- Small decorative lace medallion
- 11 metal rivets
- 2 purse straps
- Set of 4 leather buckles
- Leather buckle magnetic snap
- 4 purse feet
- 10" (25cm) long thin leather strip for inner purse
- D-ring and lobster clasp of same width as leather strip

BEFORE YOU BEGIN:

- Use a ⅜" (1cm) seam allowance unless indicated otherwise.
- Before cutting and making the front flap, please read instructions from Essential Techniques B (p. 108).
- Before making the bag, make sure to fix and mark the placement of the purse feet for the outside of the bottom of the bag. See Essential Techniques G (p. 118) for help with this.
- Find and trace the 4 pattern pieces from Side A of the pattern paper, remembering to add ⅜" (1cm) seam allowances.

CUT THE FOLLOWING PIECES FROM YOUR FABRIC AND INTERFACING:

Note that the interfacing for the bag body, sides, and flap is cut without seam allowances to reduce bulk.

- **Bag Flap:**
  - Top Layer (from pattern pack): Main outer fabric (1), Lining fabric (1), Heavyweight interfacing (1)
  - Bottom Layer (from pattern pack): Contrast fabric (1), Lining fabric (1), Heavyweight interfacing (1)
- **Bag Body** (from pattern pack): Main outer fabric (2), Lining fabric (2), Heavyweight interfacing (4)
- **Bag Sides** (from pattern pack): Contrast fabric (1), Lining fabric (1), Heavyweight interfacing (2)
- **Bag Base:**
  - Plastic Board: cut a 6⅝" x 4½" (17 x 11.5cm) rectangle
  - Plastic Board Cover – cut a 7⅞" x 5⅞" (20 x 15cm) rectangle: Lining fabric (1)
- **Outer Zipper Pocket** – cut a 9⅞" x 13⅜" (25 x 34cm) rectangle: Pocket fabric (1), Heavyweight interfacing (1)
- **Compartment Pockets:**
  - Outer Pocket – cut a 6⅜" x 12⅝" (16 x 32cm) rectangle: Pocket fabric (1), Heavyweight interfacing (1)
  - Pocket Lining – cut a 7⅛" x 12⅝" (18 x 32cm) rectangle: Lining fabric (1)
  - Three-dimensional Inner Pocket – cut a 15¾" x 9½" (40 x 24cm) rectangle: Pocket fabric (1), Heavyweight interfacing (1)

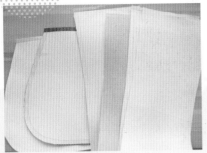

01. Iron the interfacing to the corresponding bag body and side pieces, lining it up as accurately as possible in the center of the fabric pieces.

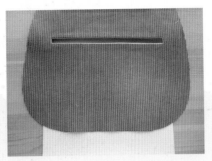

02. Refer to Essential Techniques F (p. 116) for instructions on sewing the zipper pocket. Iron the interfacing, then place the outer zipper pocket piece over the outer bag body, and sew the 8¼" x ⅜" (21 x 1cm) opening as the pattern indicates.

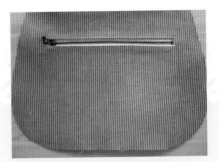

03. Line up the zipper with the opening and sew it in place.

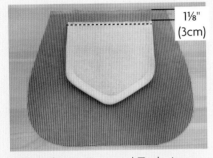

04. Refer to Essential Techniques B: Version 2 (p. 109) to create the flap. Place it face down on the bag back. Line it up 1⅛" (3cm) below the top edge, and sew it in place ¼" (0.5cm) down from the raw edge.

1⅛"
(3cm)

05. To sew the sides to the body of the bag, use small clips to fix the fabric together and curve the fabric around the bag body to form a horn-like shape.

06. Sew the fabric together where the edges match up and iron the seams. Do the same for both sides. Once finished, attach the base of the bag; see Essential Techniques G (p. 118) for more help with this. Then fold down the top edge by ⅜" (1cm).

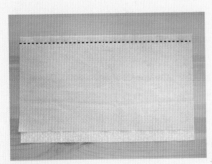

07. For the compartment pocket, sew the outer and lining pieces together along one long edge.

08. Open up the fabric pieces and iron your interfacing (trimmed to 6⅜" x 11⅞" [30 x 16cm]) on the wrong side of the outer pocket fabric. Iron the seam allowance towards the outer pocket.

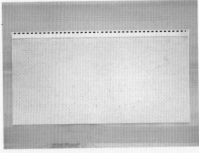

09. Fold the fabric in half with wrong sides together, and the pocket lining should peek out above the outer fabric. Edge stitch this fold.

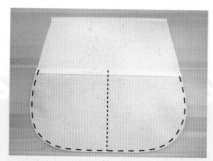

10. Line up the pocket with the bag body lining and sew a seam down the center. From the back side, baste the bag body lining to the pocket. Trim the pocket fabric to the shape of the bag when finished.

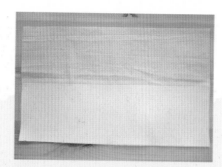

11. For the three-dimensional pocket, trim the interfacing down to 15" x 4⅜" (38 x 11cm) and iron it to the bottom half of the pocket fabric. Fold the fabric in half with wrong sides together and iron it, then baste it together along the raw edges.

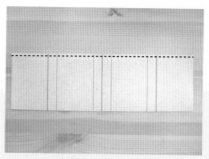

12. Mark the center line of the fabric going vertically. From this point, measure out ¾", 4", and 4¾" (2, 10, and 12cm) from each side. Mark these lines for the next step.

13. Refer to Essential Techniques D: Version 2 (p. 114) and follow the steps to use these lines to create a three-dimensional pocket, sewing pin tucks along the lines at ¾" and 4" (2 and 10cm).

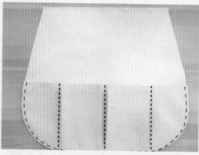

14. Line up the folded pocket on the remaining bag body lining piece and sew seams along the center and marked lines as well as all around the outer edge. Trim the excess fabric so it is shaped the same as the bag body.

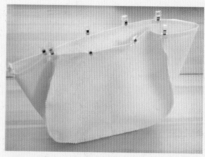

15. Sew the bag side lining to the bag body lining as in step 5, then fold under the top edges by ⅜" (1cm). The inside of the bag is all finished!

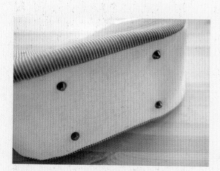

16. Attach the purse feet to the bottom of the bag.

17. Place the lining into the outer bag and sew around the entire edge. Push the lining down into the bag and hand sew any seams you like along the edges to tack the lining into place.

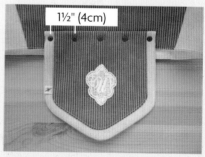

1½" (4cm)

18. Lift up the flap and attach the rivets, spaced about 1½" (4cm) apart.

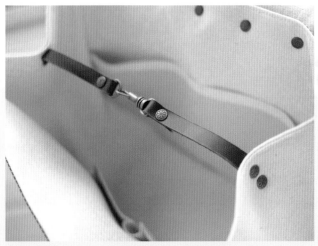

19. Attach the leather strip to the inner sides of the bag with more rivets (shown are two pieces at 4¾" [12cm] each).

20. For the final step, attach the strap and magnetic buckles, and your shoulder bag is ready to take on the go.

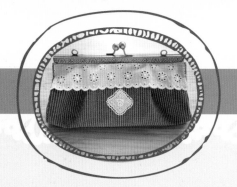

Evening Bag

The finished purse measures
9½" x 6⅝" x 3½" (24 x 17 x 9cm).

MATERIALS:

- ½ yd. (½m) of medium-weight fabric for main bag
- ½ yd. (½m) of lightweight fabric for lining
- ½ yd. (½m) of heavyweight fusible interfacing
- 7⅞" (20cm) gold metal purse frame
- 9" (23cm) length of wide decorative lace
- Small decorative lace medallion
- 25" (63.5cm) length of metal chain (optional)

BEFORE YOU BEGIN:

- Use a ⅜" (1cm) seam allowance unless indicated otherwise.
- Be sure not to leave too much extra fabric at the top edge; too much fabric can make fitting the purse frame difficult.
- Find and trace the 1 pattern piece from Side A of the pattern paper, remembering to add ⅜" (1cm) seam allowances.

CUT THE FOLLOWING PIECES FROM YOUR FABRIC AND INTERFACING:

Note that the interfacing is cut without seam allowances to reduce bulk.

- **Bag Body** – cut a 10½" x 12¼" (26.5 x 31cm) rectangle: Main outer fabric (1), Lining fabric (1), Heavyweight interfacing (2)
- **Bag Sides** (from pattern pack): Main outer fabric (2), Lining fabric (2), Heavyweight interfacing (4)

01. Iron the interfacing to the bag body, and mark the center of the bag horizontally and vertically. Sew the small medallion of decorative lace onto what will be the front of the bag.

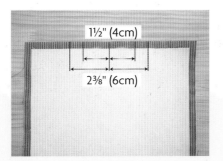

02. From the center mark you made previously, measure out 1½" (4cm) and 2⅜" (6cm) from the right and left to make folding marks. Fold over the mark at 2⅜" (6cm) to the mark at 1½" (4cm) to make pleats.

03. Repeat this with the bottom edge of your outer bag body piece and baste the pleats in place.

04. Sew the wide decorative lace onto the top edge of the outer bag body.

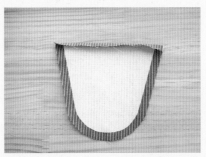

05. Iron the interfacing to the bag sides. Sew ⅜" (1cm) down from the top edge of one of your outer bag side pieces, then fold and iron the fabric toward the wrong side along this seam.

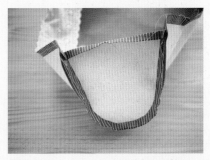

06. Line up the edge of the bag side piece with the center mark on the side of the bag body and sew the pieces together along this edge (you can trim some extra fabric from the bag body if you need to; make sure the fabric is laying flat when you do so).

07. Repeat steps 5 and 6 for the other side of the bag. When the sides are finished, sew seams ⅜" (1cm) down from the top edges of the outer bag body, then fold under and iron the fabric along the seams. Now the outside of your bag is done!

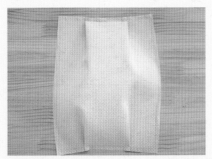

08. The instructions for making the bag lining are the same as for the outside. Repeat steps 2-3 to create the pleats.

09. Repeat steps 5-7 for the sides of the lining.

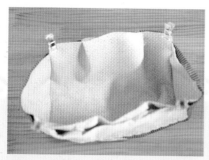  

10. Put the bag lining into the outer bag, with their wrong sides facing (the top folds should point towards the inside of the bag). Set the edges together around the mouth of the bag; you can use glue or fusible web here if it helps.

11. Edge stitch around the mouth of the bag, about ¹⁄₁₆" (0.2cm) in from the folded edges.

12. Turn the bag inside out. Pull out the center of the bag side, folding it in half. Sew a short stitch ¼" (0.5cm) in from the edge of the side fold.

13. Turn the bag back right side out and secure the gold purse frame onto the top edge of the bag. Make sure that the sides are on the inside of the frame.

14. Fasten the purse frame to the bag and you have yourself an evening bag. Play around with adding a gold or metal chain and carry your bag over your shoulder on a night out.

The finished purse measures 9⅞" x 5½" x 8⅝" (25 x 14 x 22cm).

BEFORE YOU BEGIN:

- Use a ⅜" (1cm) seam allowance unless indicated otherwise.

- Find and trace the 1 pattern piece from Side B of the pattern paper, remembering to add ⅜" (1cm) seam allowances.

CUT THE FOLLOWING PIECES FROM YOUR FABRIC AND INTERFACING:

- **Purse Body** – cut a 15" x 9½" (38 x 24cm) rectangle: Outer fabric (2), Lining fabric (2), Heavyweight interfacing (2)

- **Purse Bottom** (from pattern pack): Contrast fabric (1), Lining fabric (1)

Iron your fusible interfacing to all of the corresponding purse fabrics.

MATERIALS:

- ⅓ yd. (⅓m) of medium-weight fabric for main bag

- ¼ yd. (¼m) of complementing medium to heavyweight fabric for bottom of bag

- ⅓ yd. (⅓m) of light to medium-weight fabric for lining

- ⅓ yd. (⅓m) of heavyweight interfacing

- Small decorative cotton patch

- 2 D-rings

- Twenty ¼" (0.5cm) metal eyelets

- Leather shoulder strap

- 2 base pieces for leather strap

- About 31" (79cm) of bias tape or similar seam binding notion

- About 1 yd. (1m) of suede leather cording

- 4 metal rivets

01. Sew the cotton patch to the middle of the outer purse body front. Layer the outer purse body with its corresponding lining piece with right sides together. Sew a seam along the top edge and iron it flat. Repeat this with the remaining purse body outer fabric and lining piece.

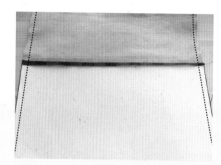

02. Take the finished pieces from the previous step and layer them over one another, matching the outer fabric to the outer fabric and the lining fabric to the lining fabric with right sides together. Sew seams along the sides of the fabric and iron the seams.

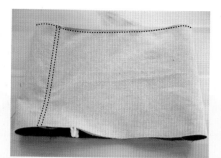

03. Turn the fabric right side out and fold it in half so the right sides of the lining fabric and the outer fabric are facing opposite directions and the right side of the lining fabric is facing you. Topstitch two rows of stitching along the side seams and edge stitch along the top seam. This finishes the purse body.

04. Layer the outer purse bottom piece and lining piece with wrong sides facing and baste the layers together.

05. Turn the purse body so the lining is facing outwards. Sew the bottom edge of the purse body entirely around the perimeter of the curved edge of the purse bottom.

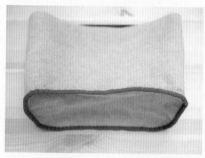

06. Bind the bottom edge of the bag with bias tape or similar seam finishing fabric. See Essential Techniques K (p. 122) for more help with this.

07. Install metal eyelets along the top edge of the purse, spaced about 1⅜" (3.5cm) apart. However, leave a wider gap in the space where the side seams are, in order for there to be room for the leather strap base.

08. Loop the D-ring through the base for the strap and fold the leather in half around the ring. Sandwich the strap base on the purse body and attach it with metal rivets.

09. Lace the suede strip through the eyelets and attach the straps to the D-rings. You have now finished your bucket purse!

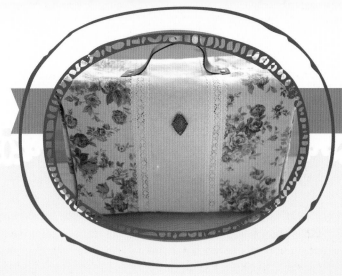

Weekend Bag

The finished case measures 8⅝" x 13" x 5½" (22 x 33 x 14cm).

Before you begin:

- Use a ⅜" (1cm) seam allowance unless indicated otherwise.

Cut the following pieces from your fabric and interfacing:

- **Case Flap:**

  - Center Panel – cut a 4⅜" x 15⅜" (11 x 39cm) rectangle: Contrast fabric (1), Heavyweight interfacing (1)

  - Side Panels – cut a 5½" x 15⅜" (14 x 39cm) rectangle: Main outer fabric (2), Heavyweight interfacing (2)

  - Flap Lining – cut a 13¾" x 15⅜" (35 x 39cm) rectangle: Lining fabric (1), Heavyweight interfacing (1)

- **Case Sides** – cut a 6¼" x 9½" (16 x 24cm) rectangle: Main outer fabric (2), Lining fabric (2), Heavyweight interfacing (4)

- **Case Front** – cut a 6¼" x 13¾" (16 x 35cm) rectangle: Contrast fabric (1), Lining fabric (1), Heavyweight interfacing (2)

- **Case Bottom** – cut a 9½" x 13¾" (24 x 35cm) rectangle: Main outer fabric (1), Lining fabric (1), Heavyweight interfacing (2)

- **Separator** – cut a 15¾" x 10¼" (40 x 26cm) rectangle: Contrast lightweight fabric (1), Heavyweight interfacing (1)

- **Case Base:**

  - Plastic Board – cut a 12¼" x 13⅜" (31 x 34cm) rectangle

  - Fabric Board Cover – cut a 13" x 14½" (33 x 37cm) rectangle: Lining fabric (1)

Materials:

- ½ yd. (½m) of medium-weight fabric for main case

- ¼ yd. (¼m) of complementing medium-weight fabric for contrasting center flap panel

- ⅔ yd. (⅔m) of lightweight fabric for lining

- ⅓ yd. (⅓m) of complementing lightweight fabric for inner separator

- 1¼ yds. (1¼m) of 44" (112cm) wide or 2 yds. (2m) of 22" (56cm) wide heavyweight interfacing

- 30" (76cm) zipper

- About 16" (40cm) of narrow decorative lace

- 1 yd. (1m) of about 1" (2.5cm) wide decorative lace

- Small decorative metal medallion

- 8¼" x 1½" (21 x 4cm) leather handle

- 4 metal rivets

01. To make the separator, trim down the interfacing to 15" x 4¾" (38 x 12cm) and iron it ⅜" (1cm) up from the bottom edge. Fold the fabric in half with right sides together and sew a seam along the bottom edge.

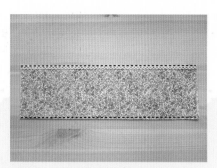

02. Turn the separator right side out and iron the fabric flat. Edge stitch along the top and bottom edges and apply the narrow decorative lace for a finishing touch.

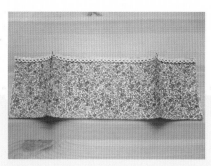

03. Measure in 3½" (9cm) from each edge and mark a vertical line across the fabric. Fold the fabric at the marks and sew pin tucks along the folds.

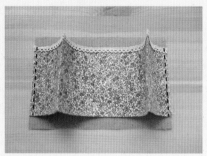

04. Line up the sides of the separator centered along the case side lining fabric. Baste the edges in place.

05. Iron the interfacing to the case side and front pieces. Sew the case front lining and remaining side to the case side piece from the previous step. When sewing, stop ⅜" (1cm) short of the bottom edge. Press the finished seam.

06. The outer case pieces are sewn similarly. Sew the case front and sides together, stopping short ⅜" (1cm) before the bottom edge.

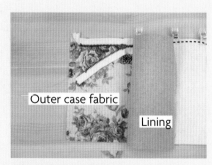

07. Find the center point of the case front, and use it to center the zipper along the top edge of the sewn case sections from the previous steps. Sew the zipper between the lining and outer case layers from steps 5 and 6 with a ¼" (0.7cm) seam allowance.

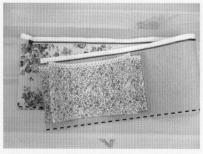

08. Flip the fabric around so the right side is now facing out. Baste along the bottom edge of the fabric to secure it.

09. Assemble the flap by sewing the center panel between the two side panels, sewing them along the long edges. Apply the wide decorative lace along the seams, and iron the interfacing to the wrong side of the fabric and the corresponding lining piece.

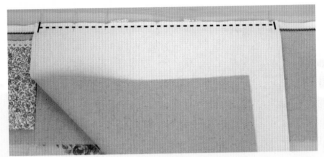

10. Find the center point of the zipper and the case flap (short side). Line them up so the case flap outer fabric and lining are centered along the case front and zipper edge. With the zipper sandwiched between the two, sew the three layers together with a ¼" (0.7cm) seam allowance, making sure not to sew past the zipper slider. The seam should be 13" (33cm) long.

11. Trim the excess zipper tape. Match up the sides of the flap with the sides of the case, creating a 90 degree angle with the zipper tape (clipping it so it pivots if necessary). Sew the layers together with a ¼" (0.7cm) seam allowance. The finished seam should be 8½" (21.5cm) long.

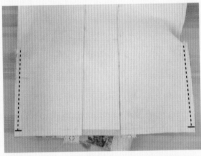

13. Turn the case right side out so outer fabric is facing outward.

12. Line up the fabric from the flap with the fabric from the case sides and sew the edges together, being sure to stop ⅜" (1cm) before the bottom edge.

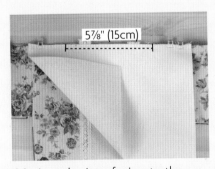

57⁄8" (15cm)

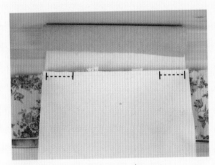

14. Iron the interfacing to the case bottom pieces, then line up the long edge of the outer fabric with the case flap and sew a 5⅞" (15cm) seam centered along the middle of the edge.

15. Line up the case bottom lining fabric along the same edge as the previous step, but from the other side with right sides facing. Sew a seam on each side of the previous seam, skipping over the seam from the previous step, but stop ⅜" (1cm) before the corners.

 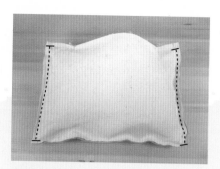 

16. Line up the case bottom and lining fabric with the case front this time, and sew along the edge, starting ⅜" (1cm) from the corner, and stopping ⅜" (1cm) before the other corner.

17. Match up the side seams in a similar manner and sew the seams the same, stopping short of the corners.

18. Using the opening that was left in step 14, turn the case right side out. Prepare the base board from the instructions in Essential Techniques G (p. 118). Insert the board into this opening, then hand sew the opening closed.

19. Zip up the zipper to close up the case.

20. Attach the 8¼" x 1½" (21 x 4cm) leather strap using the metal rivets onto the top of the cover, and attach the small metal medallion to the front of the case. Your case is now ready to fill!

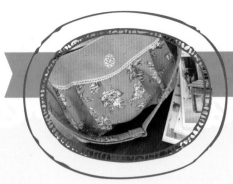

The finished purse measures 12⅝" x 9⅞" x 4" (32 x 25 x 10cm).

BEFORE YOU BEGIN:

- Use a ⅜" (1cm) seam allowance unless indicated otherwise.
- Find and trace the 3 pattern pieces from Side B of the pattern paper, remembering to add ⅜" (1cm) seam allowances.

CUT THE FOLLOWING PIECES FROM YOUR FABRIC AND INTERFACING:

Note that the interfacing is cut without seam allowances to reduce bulk.

- **Upper Purse** (from pattern pack): Contrast fabric (2), Lining fabric (2), Heavyweight interfacing (2)
- **Lower Purse** (from pattern pack): Main outer fabric (2), Lining fabric (2), Heavyweight interfacing (2)
- **Purse Bottom** (from pattern pack): Main outer fabric (1), Lining fabric (1), Heavyweight interfacing (2)
- **Purse Strap** – cut a 50" x 1¾" (127 x 4.5cm) rectangle: Outer fabric (1), Lining fabric (1), Heavyweight interfacing (1)

Iron your fusible interfacing to all of the corresponding outer purse fabrics, as well as the purse bottom lining.

MATERIALS:

- ⅓ yd. (⅓m) of medium-weight fabric for main purse
- ¼ yd. (¼m) of medium-weight complementing fabric for upper contrast panel
- ⅔ yd. (⅔m) of lightweight fabric for lining
- ⅔ yd. (⅔m) of 44" (112cm) wide or 1¼ yds. (1¼m) of 22" (56cm) wide heavyweight interfacing
- 1" (2.5cm) rectangular metal ring
- 1" (2.5cm) strap adjuster
- 50" (127cm) of 1" (2.5cm) wide webbing or similar strap fabric
- Snap button
- Small lace medallion

Instructions

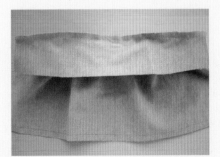

01. To make the lining, create pleats in the lining fabric by folding according to the marks on the pattern, starting from the center and going out. Baste the folds in place to secure them.

02. Line up the bottom edge of the upper purse lining with the top edge of the pleated fabric with right sides together. Sew a seam to join them together.

03. Open out the seam and press it towards the top. Top stitch along the seam just sewn, then repeat the same steps with the other lining pieces.

04. Layer the two lining pieces with right sides together, and sew them along the side edges.

05. Sew a gathering stitch around the bottom edge of the lining pieces. Gather the fabric until it is 14⅜" (36.5cm) around.

06. Sew the purse bottom lining entirely around this edge.

07. Attach the metal snap about ¾" (2cm) down from the top edge of the lining, centered horizontally. Now you have finished the inside of the purse!

08. To make the outer purse, repeat the same as for the lining with the purse bottom and top pieces. Sew the length of decorative lace along the middle seam, and sew the small lace medallion in the center to adorn the purse.

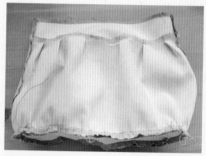

09. Continue on with steps 4-6 for the outer fabrics; you have completed the outer purse!

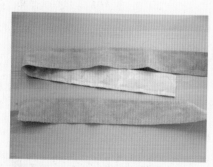

10. Layer the outer fabric and lining pieces for the strap of the purse with right sides together, and sew them along the long edges.

11. Turn the strap right side out and iron the seams. Thread the webbing through the strap tube created in the previous step, allowing the fabric to extend ⅜" (1cm) past the webbing on one end. Edge stitch the seams to secure the webbing in place.

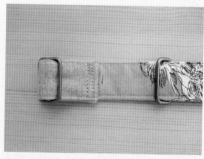

12. Using the extending ⅜" (1cm), fold the strap over the strap adjuster and sew a box stitch to secure the ⅜" (1cm) fold in place. From the other end of the strap, slip the metal ring through and trim 2⅜" (6cm) off the strap to be used next.

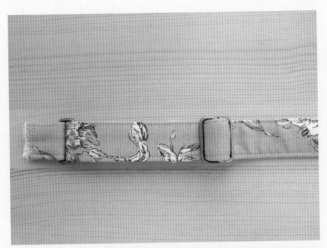

13. Loop the remaining end of the strap through the adjuster, then loop the 2⅜" (6cm) piece through the remaining end of the metal ring. Baste the ends in place to secure it. See Essential Techniques I (p. 120) for more help.

14. Line up the ends of the straps and the outer purse body along the top edges with right sides together. Line up the straps in the middle of the purse side seams and baste them in place.

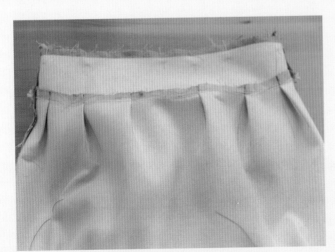

15. Place the lining into the outer purse with right sides facing, and sew a seam around the top edge of the purse, being sure to leave about a 5" (12.5cm) opening to turn the purse right side out.

16. Turn the purse right side out, then edge stitch around the top edge of the purse to sew the previous opening closed. Now you have yourself a casual purse for all of your day trips!

Lunch Bag

The finished bag measures 9⅞" x 6⅝" x 6⅜" (25 x 17 x 16cm).

MATERIALS:

- ¼ yd. (¼m) of medium-weight fabric for main bag
- ¼ yd. (¼m) of complementing medium to heavyweight fabric for bag sides and piping
- ¼ yd. (¼m) of lightweight fabric for lining
- ¼ yd. (¼m) of heavyweight interfacing
- 12" (30.5) leather strip
- Small decorative cotton patch
- Magnetic snap
- 8 metal rivets

BEFORE YOU BEGIN:

- Use a ⅜" (1cm) seam allowance unless indicated otherwise.
- Find and trace the 2 pattern pieces from Side B of the pattern paper, remembering to add ⅜" seam allowances.
- Note that you will need to fold back the Bag Bottom portion of the Bag Sides pattern piece to get the Bag Body pattern piece.

CUT THE FOLLOWING PIECES FROM YOUR FABRIC AND INTERFACING:

Note that the interfacing for the flap is cut without seam allowances to reduce bulk.

- **Bag Body** (from pattern pack): Main outer fabric (2), Lining fabric (2), Heavyweight interfacing (2)
- **Bag Sides** (from pattern pack): Contrast fabric (1), Lining fabric (1)
- **Bag Flap** (from pattern pack): Contrast fabric (1), Main outer fabric (1), Heavyweight interfacing (1)
- **Bag Piping** – cut a 19⅝" x 1⅛" (50 x 3cm) rectangle: Contrast fabric (2)

Iron your fusible interfacing to all of the corresponding bag fabrics.

01. Line up the sides of the bag body lining with the edges of the bag side lining and sew seams down the edge, stopping short ⅜" (1cm) before the end.

02. Line up the bottom edges of the bag body lining with the side fabric and sew the rest of the seam. Follow the same instructions for the other side, but leave an opening in the bottom edge.

03. Iron the seams, and trim the seam allowances. The lining part of the bag is now finished.

04. See Essential Techniques L (p. 123) for information about using the piping piece to add piping to each long edge of the bag side outer fabric. Attach the piping between the markings found on the pattern.

05. Sew the cotton patch to the center of the bag body. Sew the outer bag side pieces around the outer bag front and back, similar to the lining back in steps 1 and 2.

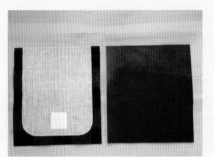

06. Iron the interfacing to the lining for the bag flap (note that the top edge requires no seam allowance). Match up the lining with the contrast flap fabric with right sides facing and sew them together along the sides and bottom. See Essential Techniques B: Version 1 (p. 108) for more help.

07. Turn the flap right side out and edge stitch along the previous seam to secure it. Attach the magnetic snap.

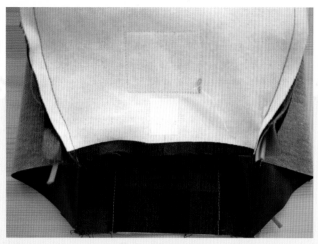

08. Align the top edge of the flap centered along the top edge of the back of the bag body. Baste the flap in place, and you've finished the outer part of the bag.

09. Place the lining into the outer bag with the right sides facing and sew a seam along the entire top edge.

10. Turn the bag right side out from the opening in the lining and edge stitch the opening closed. Also edge stitch around the opening of the bag, about ¹⁄₁₆" (0.2cm) from the top seam.

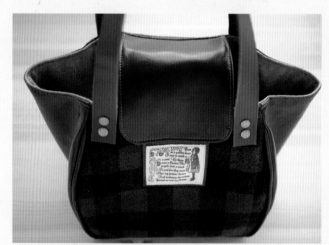

11. Trim the leather strip to two 5¾" (40cm) pieces, then attach them with rivets to the top corners of the bag. Attach the remaining half of the magnetic snap; now you have your own handmade lunch bag.

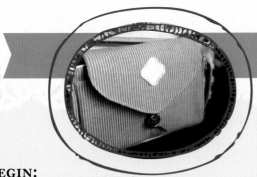

The finished purse measures 8⅝" x 5½" x 3½" (22 x 14 x 9cm).

BEFORE YOU BEGIN:

- Use a ⅜" (1cm) seam allowance unless indicated otherwise.

- Before cutting and sewing the front flap, please read Essential Techniques B: Version 1 (p. 108) to learn how to make it.

- We recommend that you baste the elastic for the elastic pockets in place to secure it. First measure your elastic to about 4½" (11cm) and trim it after both edges are sewn into place.

- Find and trace the 1 pattern piece from Side A of the pattern paper, remembering to add ⅜" (1cm) seam allowances.

CUT THE FOLLOWING PIECES FROM YOUR FABRIC AND INTERFACING:

Note that the interfacing is cut without seam allowances to reduce bulk.

- **Bag Flap** (from pattern pack): Main outer fabric (1), Lining fabric (1), Heavyweight interfacing (2)

- **Bag Body** – cut a 9½" x 6⅜" (24 x 16cm) rectangle: Main outer fabric (2), Lining fabric (2), Heavyweight interfacing (4)

- **Bag Sides** – cut a 4⅜" x 6⅜" (11 x 16cm) rectangle: Main outer fabric (2), Lining fabric (2), Heavyweight interfacing (4)

- **Bag Bottom** – cut a 9½" x 4⅜" (24 x 11cm) rectangle: Main outer fabric (1), Lining fabric (1), Heavyweight interfacing (2)

- **Outer Pockets:**

  - Elastic Side Pockets – cut a 6⅝" x 10¼" (17 x 26cm) rectangle: Main outer fabric (2), Heavyweight interfacing (1)

  - Compartment Pockets – cut a 9½" x 10¼" (24 x 26cm) rectangle: Main outer fabric (2), Heavyweight interfacing (1)

- **Inner Pockets:**

  - Side Compartment Pockets – cut a 6" x 10¼" (15 x 26cm) rectangle: Pocket fabric (2), Heavyweight interfacing (1)

  - Main Compartment Pocket – cut a 14⅛" x 10¼" (36 x 26cm) rectangle: Pocket fabric (1), Heavyweight interfacing (1)

  - Zipper Pocket – cut a 9½" x 5½" (24 x 14cm) rectangle: Pocket fabric (1), Lining fabric (1), Heavyweight interfacing (1)

  - Zipper Compartment Pocket – cut a 9½" x 7⅞" (24 x 20cm) rectangle: Pocket fabric (1), Heavyweight interfacing (1)

MATERIALS:

- ½ yd. (½m) of medium-weight fabric for outer bag

- ⅓ yd. (⅓m) of lightweight fabric for lining

- ½ yd. (½m) of complementing lightweight fabric for pockets

- 1 yd. (1m) of 44" (112cm) wide or 1⅔ yd. (1⅔m) of 22" (56cm) wide heavyweight interfacing

- Small decorative lace medallion

- 8" (20cm) zipper

- Decorative metal button

- 10" (25.5cm) of narrow elastic

- 7⅞" (20cm) strip of suede cording

- 2 small D-rings

- 6" (15cm) strip of leather

- 2 metal rivets

- Shoulder strap

01. For the outer compartment pockets, cut the interfacing in half widthwise and iron it to the bottom half of the fabric, then fold the fabric in half with wrong sides together. Baste around the edges to keep it together. Line the pocket up along the bottom edge of the main bag and baste the layers together. Follow the same instructions for the other compartment pocket.

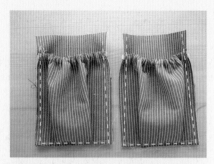

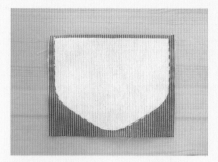

02. Refer to Essential Techniques E (p. 115) to make the elastic side pockets and baste them to the bag sides. Mark the middle point vertically across the pocket. Measure 1⅛" (3cm) out and fold this point to 2⅜" (6cm) out to create a pleat. Repeat with the other side, then baste the pleats in place.

03. Iron the interfacing to the flap of the bag. Tie a knot at one end of the strip of suede and baste it in place on the point of the bag flap with the knot facing towards the top edge of the flap. As noted in Essential Techniques B: Version 1 (p. 108), make sure that the flap lining has a ¼" (0.5cm) seam allowance along the top edge.

04. Layer the flap outer fabric and lining pieces together with right sides facing. Sew around the curved edge, then trim the seam allowances.

05. Turn the flap right side out and press it flat. Edge stitch around the curved edge of the flap.

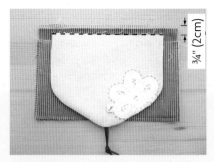

06. Layer the flap ¾" (2cm) down from the top edge of the bag body with right sides together. Sew it in place ¼" (0.5cm) down from the raw edge of the flap.

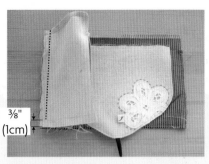

07. Layer the bag side over the bag body and sew them together, but be sure to stop ⅜" (1cm) before the bottom edge and leave an unsewn space here, as it will be sewn later. Repeat this with the other bag side and bag body pieces until you've created a square.

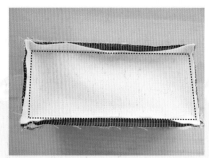

08. Iron the interfacing to the bag bottom and attach it by matching up the raw edges along the bag body and side bottom edges. Sew it in place by hand, then trim the seam allowances.

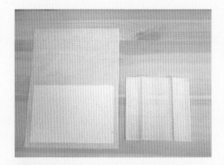

09. For the side compartment pockets, trim the interfacing to two 5⅛" x 4¾" (13 x 12cm) pieces and iron them to the bottom half of your fabric. Fold the fabric in half with wrong sides together and iron it, then baste the raw edges to hold the fabric together. Mark the center of the pocket widthwise, measure out 1⅜" (3.5cm) from each side, and make folds vertically here. Sew a pin tuck along these folds. For more help, see Essential Techniques D: Version 2 (p. 114).

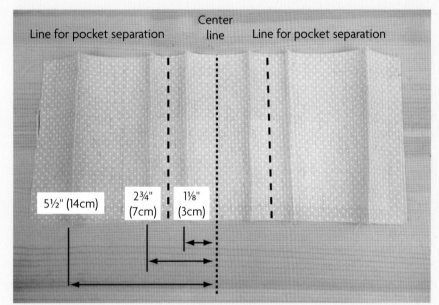

Line for pocket separation · Center line · Line for pocket separation

5½" (14cm) · 2¾" (7cm) · 1⅛" (3cm)

10. For the main inner compartment pocket, trim your interfacing to 13⅜" x 4¾" (34 x 12cm) and follow the same instructions as before. Make vertical folds 1⅛" (3cm), 2¾" (7cm), and 5½" (14cm) out from the center and sew pin tucks along these folds. At 2" (5cm) out from the center, mark a vertical line for your pocket separation.

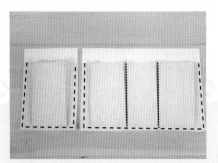

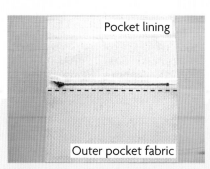

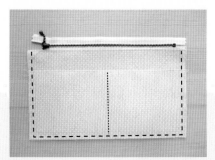

11. Line up the pockets with the bag body and side lining fabrics and fold the fabric to make the three-dimensional pockets as in Essential Techniques D: Version 2 (p. 114). Baste the pockets in place along the sides and bottom. Also sew seams along the pocket separation lines.

12. Iron the interfacing to the zipper pocket pieces. Layer the zipper between the top edges of the zipper pocket fabric and lining piece. Sew the three layers together, then edge stitch the finished seam.

13. For the zipper compartment pocket, refer to Essential Techniques C: Version 1 (p. 110). Fold the pocket in half with wrong sides together. Align it against the bottom edge of the zipper pocket and sew around the sides and bottom to hold the pocket in place; then sew along the center to create the pocket separation.

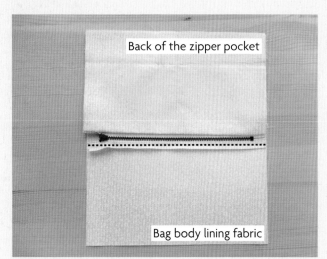

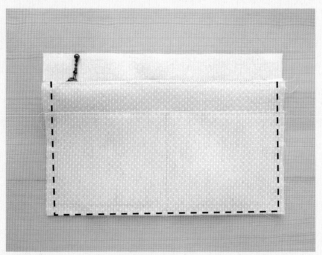

14. Take the unsewn bag body lining piece, lay it right side facing up, and layer the zipper pocket over it with right sides facing. Align the zipper tape of the zipper pocket pointing down, 1⅛" (3cm) below the top edge of the bag body lining, and sew it in place along the zipper tape.

15. Flip the zipper pocket down so the right sides are facing outward. Align the bottom edge of the zipper pocket with the bottom of the main bag lining. Baste the sides and bottom edges in place.

16. Refer back to steps 7 and 8 to complete the lining of the bag.

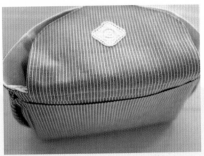

17. Fold under and iron the top edges of the outer part of the bag and the lining by ⅜" (1cm). Place the lining part of the bag into the outer part of the bag. Sew around the perimeter of the top edge. Complete the flap by folding it up and sewing it in place 5⁄16" (0.7cm) from the fold.

18. Attach the D-rings to the sides of the bag by using half of the leather strip on each side and securing it with a metal rivet.

19. Sew the button to the front of the bag, making sure that the button and suede loop from the bag flap match up.

20. The inside of the bag is now complete.

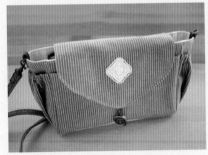

21. Attach the strap to the D-rings and clasp the flap shut. Now you have a bag to take your most important belongings with you everywhere you go!

Travel Purse

The finished purse measures 13" x 7⅞" x 4⅜" (33 x 20 x 11cm).

MATERIALS:

- ⅓ yd. (⅓m) of medium-weight fabric for main purse
- ¼ yd. (¼m) of medium-weight complementing fabric for purse sides
- 1 yd. (1m) of lightweight fabric for lining
- ½ yd. (½ yd.) of lightweight complementing fabric for inside pockets
- 1½ yds. (1½m) of 44" (112cm) wide or 2⅔ yds. (2⅔m) of 22" (56cm) wide heavyweight interfacing
- 12" (30.5cm) zipper
- 8" (20.5cm) zipper
- Two 6" (15cm) zippers
- Various decorative lace trims: 14⅛" (36cm) long (2), 5½" (14cm) long, 7" (18cm) long
- Small decorative metal medallion
- 2 magnetic snaps
- Two 1¼" (3.2cm) lobster clasps
- Two 1¼" (3.2cm) D-rings
- 1¼" (3.2cm) strap adjuster
- 1¼" (3.2cm) wide webbing or similar strapping fabric, measuring 83½" (212cm)
- Small D-ring

BEFORE YOU BEGIN:

- Use a ⅜" (1cm) seam allowance unless indicated otherwise.
- Find and trace the 2 pattern pieces from Side A of the pattern paper, remembering to add ⅜" (1cm) seam allowances.

CUT THE FOLLOWING PIECES FROM YOUR FABRIC AND INTERFACING:

Note that the interfacing is cut without seam allowances to reduce bulk.

- **Front Zipper Pockets:**
    - Top Panel (B) – cut a 14⅛" x 4" (36 x 10cm) rectangle: Contrast fabric (1), Lining fabric (1), Heavyweight interfacing (2)
    - Upper Pocket (C) – cut a 14⅛" x 1½" (36 x 4cm) rectangle: Main outer fabric (1), Heavyweight interfacing (1)
    - Pleated Pocket (D) – cut a 18⅞" x 5½" (48 x 14cm) rectangle: Main outer fabric (1), Lightweight interfacing (1)
    - Pocket Lining (E) – cut an 18⅞" x 6¼" (48 x 16cm) rectangle: Lining fabric (1)
- **Purse Body** (A) (from pattern pack): Main outer fabric (1), Lining fabric (3), Heavyweight interfacing (4)
- **Back Zipper Pocket** (F) – cut a 10⅝" x 13⅜" (27 x 34cm) rectangle: Lining fabric (1), Heavyweight interfacing (1)
- **Purse Sides** (G) (from pattern pack): Main outer fabric (1), Lining fabric (1), Heavyweight interfacing (2)
- **Small Zipper Tab** (L) – cut a 1½" x 1⅛" (4 x 3cm) rectangle: Main outer fabric (1)
- **Large Zipper Tabs** (M) – cut a 2⅜" x 1⅛" (6 x 3cm) rectangle: Main outer fabric (2)
- **Inside Pockets:**
    - Compartment Pocket Top Layer (H) – cut a 14⅛" x 12⅝" (36 x 32cm) rectangle: Pocket fabric (1), Heavyweight interfacing (1)
    - Compartment Pocket Bottom Layer (I) – cut a 14⅛" x 14⅛" (36 x 36cm) square: Pocket fabric (1), Heavyweight interfacing (1)
    - Pocket Flap (J) – cut a 5⅞" x 2¾" (15 x 7cm) rectangle: Main outer fabric (2), Pocket fabric (2), Heavyweight interfacing (2)
    - Three-dimensional Pocket (K) – cut a 15" x 10¼" (38 x 26cm) rectangle: Pocket fabric (1), Heavyweight interfacing (1)
- **D-ring Loop** – cut a 7" x 2" (18 x 5cm) rectangle: Main outer fabric (1)

Iron your fusible interfacing to all of the corresponding purse fabrics.

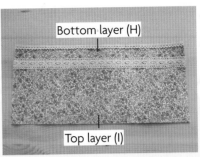

01. To make the three-dimensional pocket, refer to Essential Techniques D: Version 1 (p. 113) to prepare your fabric. Start folding and sewing pin tucks vertically throughout the pocket piece (K). Measure out and sew pin tucks 1½", 3⅛", and 6¼" (4, 8, and 16cm) to the left and right of the center. Baste these folds in place along the bottom edge.

02. Take the purse body lining (A), and line up the three-dimensional pocket (K) ¾" (2cm) above the bottom edge. Sew seams along the sides and bottom, and also between the folds to create the separating sections.

03. To make the compartment pocket, fold the top and bottom pocket layers (H and I) in half width-wise and embellish the folded edges with the 14⅛" (36cm) pieces of decorative lace. Layer the top layer (H) over the bottom layer (I) and match up the bottom raw edge. Sew a vertical seam anywhere you wish through the layers depending on your storage needs.

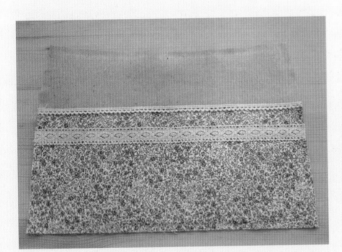

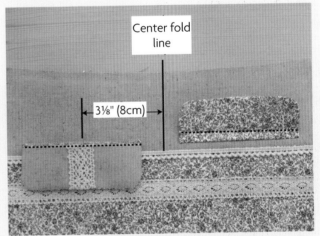

04. Line up the compartment pocket (H and I) along the bottom edge of your remaining purse body lining (A). Sew a basting seam around the edges. Refer to Essential Techniques C: Version 3 (p. 112) for more help. Trim the excess fabric to fit the shape of the purse body when finished basting.

05. To make the pocket flaps, see Essential Techniques A: Version 1 (p. 106). Embellish the outer flap pieces with the 5½" (14cm) decorative lace. From the center line of the purse body lining (A), measure out 3⅛" (8cm) and center the flap along this point. Sew it in place according to the Essential Techniques instructions. Attach the magnetic snaps; refer to Essential Techniques M (p. 124) for this.

06. Refer back to steps 18-21 of the "Compartment Clutch" to attach the D-ring onto the purse body lining (A).

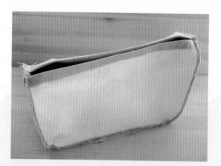

07. Fold under the top edge of the purse body lining pieces (A) by ⅜" (1cm) and iron the folds in place. Sew the purse side lining (G) along the side and bottom edges of the purse body lining. Iron the seams and trim the seam allowances when complete.

08. For the two 6" (15cm) zippers on the front of the purse, use the small zipper tab (L). Fold the short edges toward the center, then edge stitch those folds between the two zippers across the zipper tape where the zipper sliders lay.

09. For the pleated pocket (D), mark the center of the fabric piece vertically. Measure out 1⅛" (3cm) and fold this point to 2" (5cm), measure out 4⅜" (11cm) and fold it to 5⅛" (13cm), and measure out 7½" (19cm) and fold it to 8¼" (21cm). Do this on the right and left side, then baste the folds in place to create the pleats.

10. Sew this pleated edge of piece (D) to the long edge of the upper pocket (C). Then edge stitch the previous seam.

11. Create pleats on the bottom edge of piece (D) by measuring out from the center. Fold the point at 2" (5cm) to 3⅛" (8cm), and fold the point at 7⅛" (18cm) to 8¼" (21cm). Baste these folds in place to finish the pleats.

12. Repeat the pleating directions from step 9 with the pocket lining piece (E).

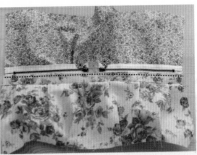

13. Layer the sewn pair of zippers between the upper pocket (C) and the pleated edge of the pocket lining (E). Sew all three layers together. Edge stitch over the previous seam to secure it.

14. On the bottom edge of the pocket lining (E), sew a gathering stitch and gather the edge to 14⅛" (36cm). Baste the gathered edge to the outer pocket fabric.

15. Line up the 7" (18cm) decorative lace vertically between the zippers and sew in place. Layer the other side of the zipper tape between the top panel (B) and its corresponding lining piece similar to step 13. Sew all three layers together, then edge stitch over the previous seam.

16. Layer the last purse body lining piece (A) (without pockets) beneath the finished zipper pocket section with both right sides facing up. Baste the two layers in place.

73

17. Sew the back zipper pocket to the outer fabric of your purse body (A) with the 8" (20.5cm) zipper and back zipper pocket (F). Refer to Essential Techniques F (p. 116) for instructions on how to do this.

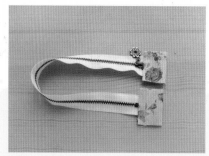

18. Take the large zipper tabs (M) and fold under the short edges by ⅜" (1cm). Wrap those folded edges around the ends of your 12" (30.5cm) zipper to create neat tabs for the ends of your zipper.

19. Sew the top edges of your outer purse body (A) to one side of the zipper tape. Repeat this with the other side of the zipper tape and the top edge of the double zipper pocket section.

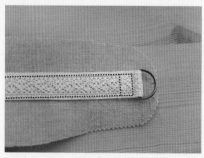

20. To create the side strap, cut 28⅜" (72cm) from your length of webbing, loop each end through a D-ring and fold it under by 1⅛" (3cm). Layer the entire strap centered over the outer purse sides piece (G) and sew around the perimeter of the strap to anchor it in place.

21. Similar to step 7, sew the outer purse sides (G) to the purse body (A) by wrapping the side pieces around the sides and bottom of the body pieces and sewing them in place. You are now finished with the outer part of the purse.

22. Put the lining into the outer purse with wrong sides together. Line up the folded edges in the lining with the zipper tape, then hand sew it in place around the mouth of the purse.

23. Refer to Essential Techniques I (p. 120) to create the adjustable strap with the remaining 55 ⅛" (140cm) of your strap material. Latch the strap to the D-rings of the purse, and sew on the decorative metal medallion to the front. Adjust the length to whatever is most comfortable for you, and take your new purse out on the road.

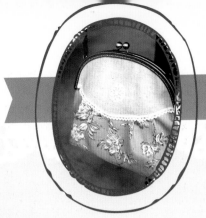

*The finished purse measures
10" x 8½" x 2½" (25 x 22 x 6cm).*

BEFORE YOU BEGIN:

- Use a ⅜" (1cm) seam allowance unless indicated otherwise.

- When choosing the cord for the strap of your purse, make sure to pay attention to the strength of the material, and avoid decorative straps, which will easily crack open and possibly break.

- Find and trace the 3 pattern pieces from Side B of the pattern paper, remembering to add ⅜" (1cm) seam allowances.

CUT THE FOLLOWING PIECES FROM YOUR FABRIC AND INTERFACING:

- **Top Contrast Panel** (from pattern pack): Contrast fabric (1), Medium-weight interfacing (1)

- **Bottom Front** (from pattern pack): Main outer fabric (1), Medium-weight interfacing (1)

- **Purse Body** (from pattern pack): Main outer fabric (1), Medium-weight interfacing (1), Lining fabric (2)

- **Purse Bottom** – cut a 9½" x 3⅛" (24 x 8cm) rectangle: Complementing bottom fabric (1), Medium-weight interfacing (1), Lining fabric (1)

MATERIALS:

- ¼ yd. (¼m) of complementing medium-weight fabric for top panel

- ¼ yd. (¼m) of medium-weight fabric for main purse

- ¼ yd. (¼m) of light to medium-weight fabric for lining

- ¼ yd. (¼m) of 44" (112cm) wide or ½ yd. (½m) of 22" (56cm) wide medium-weight fusible interfacing

- ⅛ yd. (⅛m) of complementing medium-weight fabric for bottom of purse

- 7⅞" (20cm) metal purse frame

- 10" (23cm) of narrow decorative lace

- 25" (63.5cm) thin leather cording for strap

- Small decorative lace medallion

Instructions

01. Iron the interfacing to the bottom front of your outer fabric (note that the top edge should have the seam allowance cut off). Following the marks on the pattern, fold the fabric outward towards the designated points to create pleats. Baste the pleats in place.

02. Iron the interfacing to the top contrast panel of your purse and sew it to the bottom by layering the edges over one another with both right sides facing up. To hide the raw edge, sew the lace in place to cover the edge. Also sew the small lace medallion in the center; this will be the outer front side of your purse.

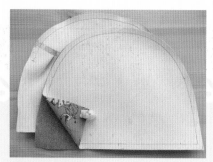

03. Line up the purse's outer fabric and lining, right sides facing towards one another, and sew a seam along the top edge between the guidelines marked by the pattern.

04. Iron the interfacing to the purse bottom and center it along the bottom edge of the outer purse body fabric. Sew the edges together, but start ⅜" (1cm) from the edge and end ⅜" (1cm) short of the edge.

05. Repeat this with the other side of the purse bottom and the remaining piece for the outer purse body.

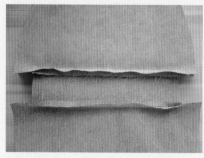

06. Repeat steps 4 and 5 for the lining of the purse. But in step 5, leave about a 5" (13cm) gap in the middle of the seam open.

07. Fold the purse in half along the middle of the purse bottom so the unsewn purse body side edges meet each other with outer fabric facing outer fabric. Sew these edges together, then repeat this with the lining part of the purse. Press the seams open when complete. Line up the side edges of the purse bottom with the remaining raw edge along the purse body, then sew across those edges, completing the bottom of the purse.

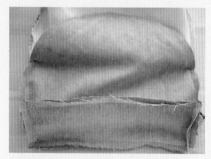

08. Repeat sewing the bottom corners for the lining portion of the purse.

09. From the opening in the bottom of the lining, turn the purse right side out and edge stitch the opening closed.

10. Sew on the gold purse frame. Then loop the leather cording through the holes on both sides and secure them. You have now finished your vintage-style purse.

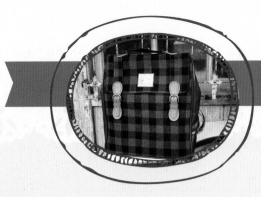

The finished bag measures 11¾" x 13" x 3½" (30 x 33 x 9cm).

BEFORE YOU BEGIN:

- Use a ⅜" (1cm) seam allowance unless indicated otherwise.

- Before cutting and making the front flap, please read Essential Techniques B: Version 1 (p. 108). Note that the top edge of the outer fabric has only a ¼" (0.5cm) seam allowance while the top edge of the lining fabric has no seam allowance.

- If you would like the bag to be more firm and stiff, you can iron on an extra layer of heavy interfacing without a seam allowance.

- Find and trace the 1 pattern piece from Side A of the pattern paper, remembering to add ⅜" (1cm) seam allowances.

CUT THE FOLLOWING PIECES FROM YOUR FABRIC AND INTERFACING:

Note that the interfacing is cut without seam allowances to reduce bulk.

- **Bag Flap** (from pattern pack): Main outer fabric (1), Lining fabric (1), Heavyweight interfacing (2)

- **Handle** – cut a 3" x 9⅞" (7.5 x 25cm) rectangle: Main outer fabric (1)

- **Flap Strips** – cut a 2" x 7½" (5 x 19cm) rectangle: Main outer fabric (2), Heavyweight interfacing (2)

- **Bag Body** – cut a 12⅝" x 13¾" (32 x 35cm) rectangle: Main outer fabric (2), Lining fabric (2), Heavyweight interfacing (2)

- **Bag Sides** – cut a 38½" x 4⅜" (98 x 11cm) rectangle: Contrast fabric (1), Lining fabric (1)

- **Bottom Interfacing** – cut a 12⅝" x 4⅜" (32 x 11cm) rectangle: Heavyweight interfacing (1)

- **Outer Pocket** – cut a 12⅝" x 13⅜" (32 x 34cm) rectangle: Main outer fabric (1), Lining fabric (1), Heavyweight interfacing (1)

- **Inner Pocket** – cut a 12⅝" x 13⅜" (32 x 34cm) rectangle: Lining fabric (4), Heavyweight interfacing (2)

- **Front Piping** – cut a 37¾" x 1⅛" (96 x 3cm) rectangle: Contrast fabric (1)

MATERIALS:

- ½ yd. (½m) of 55" (140cm) wide or ⅔ yd. (⅔m) of 44" (112cm) wide medium-weight fabric for main bag

- ¼ yd. (¼m) of complementing medium to heavyweight fabric for sides and piping

- 1¼ yds. (1¼m) of lightweight fabric for lining

- 1 yd. (1m) of 44" (112cm) wide or 1½ yds. (1½m) of 22" (56cm) wide heavyweight interfacing

- 2 magnetic snap buckles

- Small decorative cotton patch

- 2 adjustable leather straps

- 5 leather strap bases

- 3 D-rings

- 2 rectangular metal rings

- 2 metal snaps

- 17 metal rivets

- 9" (23cm) webbing or similar strapping material

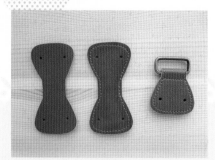

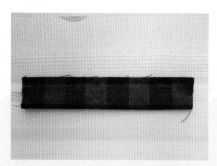

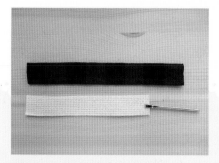

01. Edge stitch around the base pieces for the straps with a long stitch for leather. Fold the leather in half around the square metal ring, and sew a straight seam under the ring.

02. Iron the interfacing to the handle piece, then take the strap and fold it in half lengthwise with right sides together. Sew down this long edge and iron the seam.

03. Turn the tube right side out, then thread the webbing through the tube, centering it so the excess fabric extends from each side.

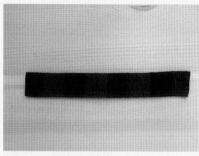

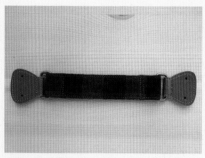

04. Edge stitch around the perimeter of the handle to anchor the webbing in place.

05. Loop the handle through the square metal rings, folding the excess strap fabric inward, then sew a box stitch to anchor the fabric in place.

06. Create the inner pockets by first ironing the interfacing, then sewing the lining pieces together along the top long edge. Turn the fabric right side out and press the pockets flat. Line them up along the bottom edges of the bag body lining fabrics and baste them in place. See Essential Techniques C: Version 3 (p. 112) for more help with this.

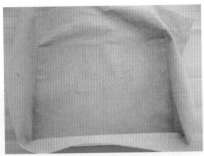

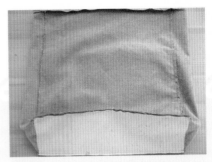

07. Find the center point of the bag side lining widthwise, and iron the interfacing centered along this point. Sew the bag sides around the bag body along the side and bottom edges.

08. Press the seam allowance towards the sides of the bag, then top stitch it in place.

09. Repeat this with the other side of the bag side lining. When complete, sew along the top edge of the bag lining with a ½" (1.2cm) seam allowance. Fold the fabric along this seam line and iron it.

10. Prepare the outer pocket similarly to the inner pocket, and attach one half of the magnetic snap. Iron the interfacing to the outer bag body back and attach the other half of the snap. Then baste the outer pocket in place by lining up the bottom raw edge. See Essential Techniques M (p. 124) for more help with the magnetic snap.

11. For the flap strips, trim the interfacing to 1⅛" x 6⅝" (3 x 17cm) and iron it to your fabric. Fold the strips in half lengthwise with right sides together and sew them along the long edge. Turn them right side out and iron them flat.

12. Iron the interfacing to the bag flap pieces, then layer the strips over the flap outer fabric by lining them up 3⅛" (8cm) out from the center of the flap piece. Edge stitch them in place. Also apply the decorative cotton patch.

13. Layer the flap outer fabric and lining together with right sides facing. Sew the two layers together along the sides and bottom. See Essential Techniques B: Version 1 (p. 108) for more help.

14. Trim the seam allowances, turn the flap right side out, and iron it flat. Sew a final edge stitch around the finished seam to secure it.

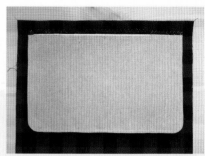

15. With right sides facing each other, layer the flap piece over the back side of the bag body. Leave the flap facing downward and line up the raw edge 1⅜" (3.5cm) down from the top edge of the bag body. Sew the flap in place here.

16. Attach the top half of the magnetic snap buckles at the bottom of the bag flap.

17. See Essential Techniques L (p. 123) to use your piping piece to create piping for the main bag front. Apply it around the sides and bottom. After this, sew the bottom half of the leather buckle snaps onto the bag body front. Sew around the leather border to secure them in place.

18. Sew the outer bag sides to the bag front similarly to step 7.

19. Repeat this for the other side and you have finished the outer part of the bag. Fold under ½" (1.2cm) along the top edge of the bag as with the lining.

20. Put the lining into the outer bag with wrong sides together and edge stitch around the top edge of the bag. Lift up the flap and attach the metal rivets.

21. Loop the D-rings through the leather base pieces, then attach them to the bottom corners and center top of the bag back with more metal rivets.

22. Attach the top handle to the bag flap with more metal rivets.

23. Install the metal snaps on the sides of the bag. Install the prong side towards the front corner and the socket side towards the back corner.

24. You can now attach the straps, fill your school bag, and head to class.

Compartment Clutch

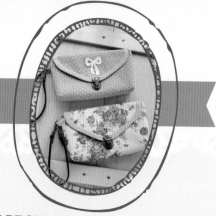

The finished clutch measures 7½" x 4¾" x 1½" (19 x 12 x 4cm).

MATERIALS:

- ¼ yd. (¼m) of medium-weight fabric for main clutch
- ⅓ yd. (⅓m) of lightweight fabric for lining
- ⅓ yd. (⅓m) of 44" (112cm) wide or ⅔ yd. (⅔m) of 22" (56cm) wide heavyweight interfacing
- ⅓ yd. (⅓m) of ultra-firm interfacing
- 7" (18cm) zipper
- 4¾" (12cm) of wide decorative lace
- ½" (1.3cm) D-ring
- Push-lock style clasp
- 13" (32.5cm) of bias binding or bias fabric for folding your own
- Leather wrist strap

BEFORE YOU BEGIN:

- Use a ⅜" (1cm) seam allowance unless indicated otherwise.
- Find and trace the 1 pattern piece from Side A of the pattern paper. Note that this piece needs no seam allowances along any edge.

CUT THE FOLLOWING PIECES FROM YOUR FABRIC AND INTERFACING:

- **Clutch Body** – cut a 9¾" x 6" (25 x 15cm) rectangle: Main outer fabric (2), Lining fabric (2), Heavyweight interfacing (2), Ultra-firm interfacing (2)
- **Card Pocket** – cut a 7⅞" x 3½" (20 x 9cm) rectangle: Lining fabric (2), Heavyweight interfacing (1)
- **Zipper Pocket** – cut an 8¼" x 4⅜" (21 x 11cm) rectangle: Lining fabric (4), Heavyweight interfacing (4)
- **Flap** (from pattern pack): Main outer fabric (1), Lining fabric (1), Heavyweight interfacing (2)
- **D-ring Loop** – cut a 7" x 2" (18 x 5cm) rectangle: Main outer fabric (1)

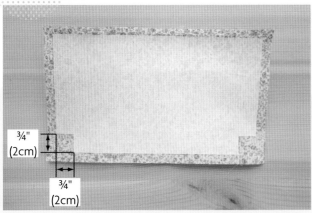

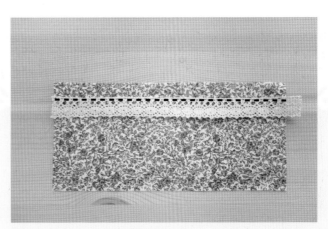

01. Trim the interfacing for the clutch body pieces to 9" x 5⅛" (23 x 13cm). From each bottom corner, trim away a square that is ¾" x ¾" (2 x 2cm). When this is complete, iron the interfacing to the corresponding clutch body fabric pieces.

02. For the card pocket, trim the interfacing pieces to 7" x 2¾" (18 x 7cm) and iron them to the fabric. Sew on a strip of decorative lace to the top, about ⅜" (1cm) down from the top edge.

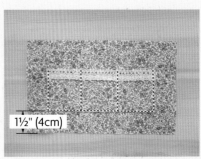

03. Face the right sides of the card pocket pieces together and sew around the entire edge of the fabric, leaving a small opening in the bottom. See Essential Techniques C: Version 2 (p. 111) for more help.

04. Turn the pocket right side out from the opening, and iron it flat. Edge stitch along the top edge of the lace to secure the edge. The card pocket is almost complete.

05. Layer the completed card pocket onto the lining for the clutch body, lining it up 1½" (4cm) up from the bottom edge. Sew it in place along the sides and bottom, then sew vertical lines throughout the pocket at 2⅜" (6cm) intervals. This completes the card pocket.

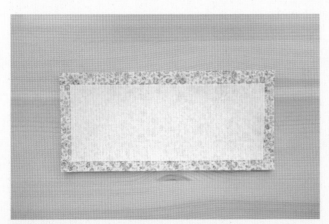

06. To create the zipper pocket, begin by trimming the interfacing to 7½" x 3½" (19 x 9cm). Iron it in place. This will be the fabric for the outside of the pocket.

07. Sandwich the zipper between the outer and inner zipper pocket fabric pieces, and sew the three layers together. Press the fabric away from the zipper and edge stitch the previous seam.

08. Repeat this for the other side of the zipper and the remaining zipper pocket pieces.

09. Fold the pocket with the outer pieces facing out and baste the raw edges together.

10. Line up the bottom edge of the zipper pocket with the lining of the clutch body.

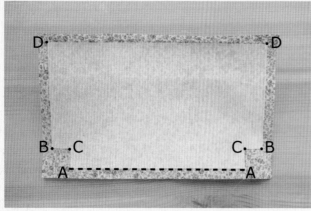 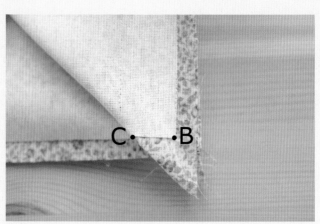

11. Take the remaining clutch body lining, and layer it over the pieces from step 10 as seen in the picture above. Note the letter markings for the different points on the fabric. On the bottom edge, sew a seam between the two points marked A.

12. Take the side with point B and fold it down to meet point A.

 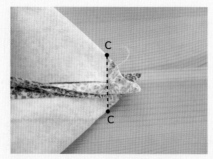 

13. While the fabric is folded as such, sew a seam from point D to point B, keeping in mind that this will also sew over the edges of the zipper pocket in the middle.

14. Spread out the fabric from the bottom corner and sew a seam between the C points.

15. Sew around the top edge of the lining, using a ⅜" (1cm) seam allowance. Then use that seam to fold under the top edge and iron it in place. The lining of the clutch is now complete.

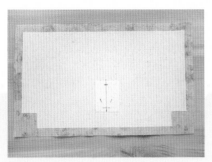

16. To make the outside of the clutch, add another small swatch of interfacing where the push-lock clasp will be installed. Make sure to mark this point.

17. Install the clasp at this point, lining it up depending on the dimensions of your particular clasp. See Essential Techniques M (p. 124) for more help with this.

18. Take your D-ring loop and pass it through a ½" (1.5cm) bias tape maker. Iron the folds as they come out of the bias tape maker.

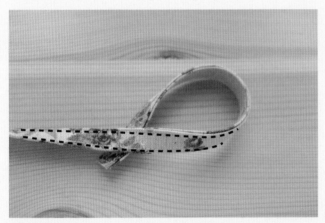

19. With the strip folded in half with wrong sides together, edge stitch along both long sides.

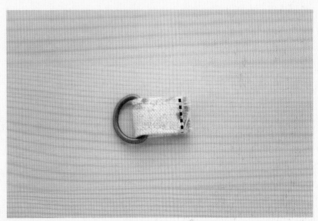

20. Trim 1½" (4cm) of the strip, and use this bit to wrap around the D-ring. Baste the ends of the strip together.

21. Baste it to one upper corner of the outer clutch body, sewing it ¾" (2cm) down from the top edge.

22. Iron the interfacing to the clutch flap pieces, then line up the flap outer fabric and lining with wrong sides together. Refer to Essential Techniques K (p. 122) to attach bias binding to the bottom edge of the flap.

23. Baste the flap to the back of the clutch body, lining up the edge with the top edge of the clutch depending on the dimensions of your clasp.

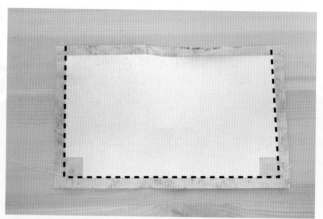

24. Layer the outer clutch body pieces together with right sides facing, and sew them along the sides and bottom.

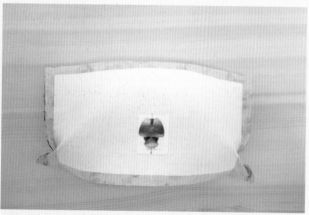

25. Sew the corners similar to step 14, then flip the clutch right side out. Fold under the top edge by ⅜" (1cm) as in step 15. You have finished the outer part of the clutch.

26. Put the lining portion from step 15 into the outer clutch, then sew together the folded edges to secure the top opening of the clutch.

27. Attach the push-lock clasp and the wrist strap, and you have finished your compartment clutch.

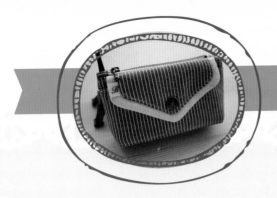

Chic Coin Purse

The finished purse measures 5½" x 2¾" x 1⅛" (14 x 7 x 3cm).

BEFORE YOU BEGIN:

- Use a ⅜" (1cm) seam allowance unless indicated otherwise.

- Find and trace the 4 pattern pieces from Side A of the pattern paper, remembering to add ⅜" (1cm) seam allowances.

- Before making the purse flap, refer to Essential Techniques A: Version 2 (p. 107), noting the seam allowance requirements for the top edge.

CUT THE FOLLOWING PIECES FROM YOUR FABRIC AND INTERFACING:

Note that the interfacing is cut without seam allowances to reduce bulk.

- **Flap Top Layer** (from pattern pack): Main outer fabric (1), Lining fabric (1), Heavyweight interfacing (1)

- **Flap Bottom Layer** (from pattern pack): Lining fabric (2), Heavyweight interfacing (1)

- **Outer Pocket** (from pattern pack): Main outer fabric (2), Heavyweight interfacing (1)

- **Purse Body** (from pattern pack): Main outer fabric (2), Lining fabric (2), Heavyweight interfacing (4)

- **Zipper Tabs** – cut a 1⅜" x 1½" (3.5 x 4cm) rectangle: Main outer fabric (2), Heavyweight interfacing (2)

MATERIALS:

- ⅛ yd. (⅛m) of light to medium-weight fabric for main purse

- ⅛ yd. (⅛m) of lightweight fabric for lining

- ¼ yd. (¼m) of 44" (112cm) wide or ⅓ yd. (⅓m) of 22" (56cm) wide heavyweight interfacing

- 3" (7.5cm) zipper

- Metal snap

- Monogrammed ribbon

Instructions

01. First, refer to Essential Techniques A: Version 2 (p. 107) for steps on making the purse flap.

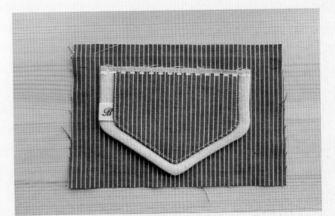

02. From the bottom corners of the bag body interfacing pieces, trim away a ¾" x ¾" (2 x 2cm) square, then iron the interfacing to the purse body pieces. Align the top edge of the flap ¾" (2cm) down from the top edge of the outer purse body. Sew the flap ¼" (0.5cm) down from the raw edge.

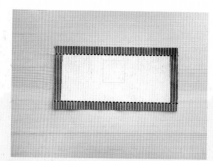

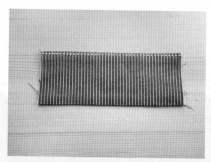

03. Lift up the flap and sew it down again ⁵⁄₁₆" (0.7cm) away from the previous seam.

04. Iron the interfacing to the outside pocket fabric, and layer it with the remaining outside pocket piece, right sides facing. Sew them together along the top and bottom edges. When finished, iron another layer of interfacing in the center, as this is where the button will be attached.

05. Turn the pocket right side out and edge stitch it along the top edge, securing the previous seam.

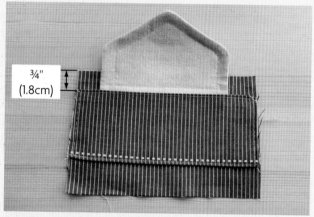

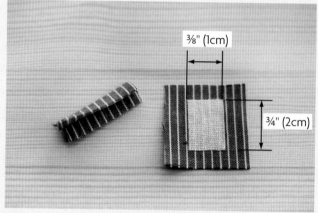

06. Line up the pocket beneath the flap on the outer purse body. Align it ¾" (1.8cm) beneath the top edge, then sew the pocket in place with an edge stitch along the bottom edge.

07. For the zipper tabs, trim the interfacing to ⅜" x ¾" (1 x 2cm) and iron it in place. Fold the short ends inward by ⅜" (1cm) and iron them. Then fold the entire tab in half with wrong sides together and iron it again.

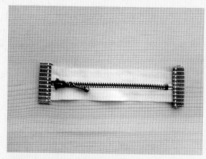

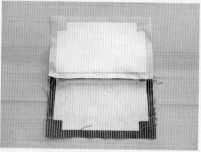

08. Trim the excess zipper tape at the ends to ⅜" (1cm). Wrap the tabs around the ends of the zipper tape and edge stitch them in place.

09. Taking the outer purse body from step 6, fold under the top edge by ⅜" (1cm). Using fusible web tape, iron the folded edge of the purse body to one side of the zipper tape, fusing it in place.

10. Turn the fabric over and line up the purse body lining along the other side of the zipper tape. Iron it in place with fusible web tape as well.

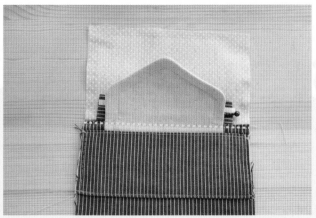

11. Lift the flap, then edge stitch along the folded edge across the zipper tape. Make sure the lining is folded out when you do this.

12. Repeat the previous steps for the other side of the zipper tape. Then apply the metal snap to the bottom of the flap and the pocket.

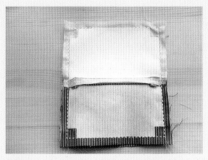

13. Line up the raw edges of the purse body pieces, facing the outer fabric to outer fabric and lining fabric to lining fabric, right sides together. Sew around the entire edge, leaving a small opening in the lining.

14. Pull the corners together to make a triangle and sew a seam across (using the interfacing as a guide), making the purse three-dimensional.

15. Turn the purse right side out from the opening in the lining, then sew the opening closed.

16. You have finished your chic and classy coin purse!

Classy Clutch

The finished clutch measures 7" x 4" x ⅜" (18 x 10 x 1cm).

MATERIALS:

- ⅛ yd. (⅛m) of light to medium-weight complementing fabric contrast top panel
- ¼ yd. (¼m) of light to medium-weight fabric for main clutch
- ¼ yd. (¼m) of lightweight fabric for lining
- 6" (15.5cm) zipper
- 8" (20.5cm) of narrow decorative lace
- Small medallion of decorative lace

BEFORE YOU BEGIN:

- Use a ⅜" (1cm) seam allowance unless indicated otherwise.
- Find and trace the 4 pattern pieces from Side B of the pattern paper, remembering to add ⅜" (1cm) seam allowances.

CUT THE FOLLOWING PIECES FROM YOUR FABRIC:

- **Top Contrast Panel** (from pattern pack): Contrast fabric (1)
- **Clutch Body** (from pattern pack): Main outer fabric (2)
- **Clutch Lining** (from pattern pack): Lining fabric (2)
- **Inner Clutch** (from pattern pack): Main outer fabric (2), Lining fabric (2)
- **Inner Pocket** – cut a 6⅜" x 3½" (16 x 9cm) rectangle: Main outer fabric (1), Lining fabric (1)
- **Zipper Tabs** – cut a 1½" x 1⅛" (4 x 3cm) rectangle: Main outer fabric (2)

01. Layer the contrast panel over the outer clutch body fabric with both right sides facing up. Edge stitch it in place, apply the decorative lace to cover the raw edge, and sew on the lace medallion in the middle. Bring together the marks on the corner of the outer clutch body and sew them in place to make small pleats.

02. Fold under the two short edges of the zipper tabs by ⅜" (1cm), then wrap the folded edges around each end of the zipper and sew them in place. Layer the zipper tape between the outer clutch body and the clutch lining, matching up the top edges and zipper tape. Sew these three layers together.

03. Layer the fabric for the inner clutch and its corresponding lining piece together with right sides facing. Sew them together along the top edge. Turn the fabric right side out and iron the seam flat. Repeat this with the remaining inner clutch pieces.

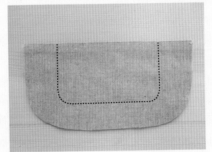

04. Layer the two inner clutch pieces with outer fabrics facing each other. Sew them together along the seam line indicated on the pattern. This completes the inner clutch.

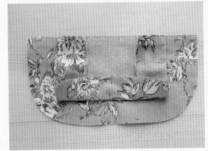

05. Fold the first two layers of the inner clutch piece back against the seam you have just sewn. Pin it in place so that the last two layers of inner clutch fabric are unobstructed.

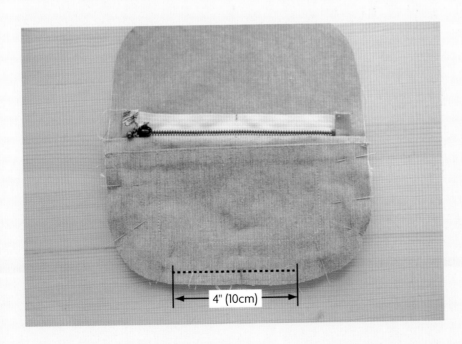

4" (10cm)

06. Take the outer clutch body from step 2 and layer it under the inner clutch piece so that the outer fabrics are facing each other. Line up the bottom edge, then sew the layers together across a 4" (10cm) length centered along the bottom of the clutch.

07. Wrap the clutch lining back around to the other side of the clutch and match up the raw edges. Sew it in place along edges that were not covered in the previous step, skipping over the 4" (10cm) section on the bottom.

08. Trim the seam allowance and turn the clutch right side out from the opening in the bottom. Sew the opening closed.

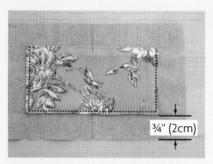

¾" (2cm)

09. Refer to Essential Techniques C: Version 1 (p. 110) to make the inner pocket. Sew it in place ¾" (2cm) up from the bottom edge of the clutch lining.

10. Line up the outer clutch body and clutch lining along the remaining side of the zipper tape, sandwiching the zipper between the two layers. Sew the three layers together.

11. Layer the clutch outer fabrics over each other with right sides facing, then repeat steps 6-8 with these fabric pieces and the remaining clutch lining that is still attached to the zipper.

12. Sew the opening closed as before. Now you have your own classy handmade clutch.

The finished notebook measures 6" x 8⅝" (15 x 22cm), which will fit an A5 sized notebook.

BEFORE YOU BEGIN:

- Use a ⅜" (1cm) seam allowance unless indicated otherwise.
- Find and trace the 3 pattern pieces from Side A of the pattern paper, remembering to add ⅜" (1cm) seam allowances.

CUT THE FOLLOWING PIECES FROM YOUR FABRIC AND INTERFACING:

Note that the interfacing is cut without seam allowances to reduce bulk.

- **Outer Notebook:**
    - Center Panel – cut a 9⅞" x 9½" (25 x 24cm) rectangle: Main outer fabric (1)
    - Side Panels – cut a 7½" x 9½" (19 x 24cm) rectangle: Contrast fabric (2)
- **Notebook Lining** – cut a 23¼" x 9½" (59 x 24cm) rectangle: Lining fabric (1)
- **Large Pocket** (from pattern pack): Main outer fabric (2), Lining fabric (2)
- **Small Pocket:**
    - Center Pocket Panel – cut a 3½" x 3⅛" (9 x 8cm) rectangle: Main outer fabric (1)
    - Side Pocket Panels – cut a 1½" x 3⅛" (4 x 8cm) rectangle: Contrast fabric (2)
    - Pocket Lining (from pattern pack): Lining fabric (1)
    - Pocket Flap (from pattern pack): Contrast fabric (1), Lining fabric (1), Heavyweight interfacing (2)
- **Card Holder** – cut a 4" x 5⅞" (10 x 15cm) rectangle: Main outer fabric (1), Lining fabric (1)

MATERIALS:

- ⅓ yd. (⅓m) of light to medium-weight fabric for main notebook and pockets
- ⅓ yd. (⅓m) of light to medium-weight complementing fabric for notebook side panels
- ⅓ yd. (⅓m) of lightweight fabric for lining
- ⅛ yd. (⅛m) of heavyweight interfacing
- 4" (10cm) leather strip
- ⅔ yd. (⅔m) of decorative lace
- 4" (10cm) of wide decorative lace for pocket flap
- Leather strap with snap
- 2" (5cm) of cotton ribbon

01. Line up the contrast center panel with the side panels for the outer notebook along the 9½" (24cm) long edges. Sew them together along these edges to create one long strip with the center panel in the middle. Apply the decorative lace along the seams.

02. For the large pockets, refer to Essential Techniques C: Version 2 (p. 111). When the pockets are complete, edge stitch the pockets along the slanted edges. Sew on the strips of leather, one horizontally about 1 ⅛" (3cm), the other strip vertically about 2 ¾" (7cm) as the picture illustrates.

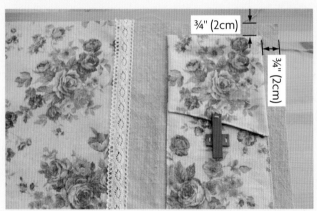

03. Take the bottom part of the large pocket and line it up on the right side of the notebook fabric from step 1. Line it up ¾" (2cm) up and to the left of the bottom right corner, then edge stitch it in place along the sides and bottom.

04. Layer the top part of the large pocket in line above the bottom part (¾" [2cm] down and to the left of the upper right corner) and edge stitch it in place along the top. You have finished the large pocket!

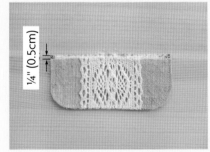

05. For the outside of the small pocket, sew the center pocket panel to the side panels along the 3⅛" (8cm) edges. This should create a strip with the center panel between the two side panels. Use the pocket paper pattern as a template to cut this fabric to the proper pocket shape.

06. Layer the outer pocket fabric over the lining with right sides together, then refer to Essential Techniques C: Version 2 (p. 111) to complete the pocket. Turn the pocket right side out and edge stitch it along the top edge.

07. Apply the wide lace to the outer pocket flap fabric, then refer to Essential Techniques A: Version 1 (p. 106) to finish the flap for the small pocket. Iron interfacing to the lining fabric to make it stiffer.

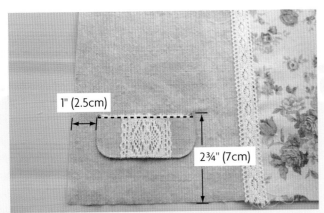

08. Take the flap with the outer side facing up and layer it over the left side of the fabric from step 1. Line it up 1" (2.5cm) to the right and 2¾" (7cm) up from the bottom left corner. Sew the flap in place ¼" (0.5cm) down from the raw edge.

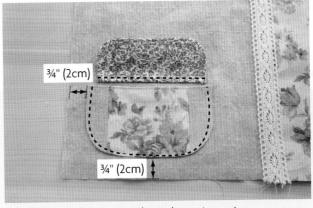

09. Flip the flap upwards and sew it again, 5/16" (0.7cm) up from the previous seam to secure it. Sew the pocket in place as well, edge stitching it ¾" (2cm) to the right and up from the bottom left corner.

10. For the card holder, apply some of the excess lace to the outer fabric corner if desired. Layer the outer fabric and lining pieces with right sides facing and matching up the raw edges. Take the cotton ribbon, folded in half, and baste it in place at the upper right corner between the outer fabric and lining for the card holder.

11. Make the card holder following the instructions on Essential Techniques C: Version 2 (p. 111). When complete, turn the pocket right side out and edge stitch the left edge to secure it.

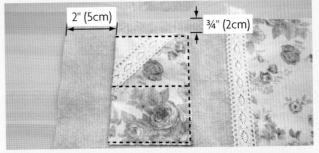

12. Line up the pocket on the left side of the outer notebook fabric, 2" (5cm) to the right and ¾" (2cm) down from the upper left corner. Edge stitch it in place along the top, right, and bottom edges, then sew another seam horizontally along the center to separate the two sections.

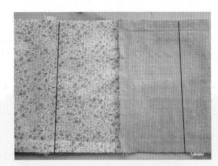

13. Layer the outer notebook fabric over the inner fabric with right sides together. Sew them together along the left and right sides. On one of the sides, leave a 4" (10cm) space in the middle of the seam, then iron the seams.

14. On the wrong side of the fabric, measure out 5½" (14cm) to the left and right of the seam from the previous step, and make vertical lines along these marks. These will be used as folding lines for the next step.

15. From the marked folding lines, fold the fabric inward to create a kind of ∑ shape.

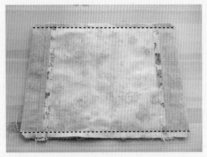

16. After folding the fabric, flatten the layers and sew along the upper and lower edges of the fabric. Trim the seam allowances at the corners, being sure not to cut through the seam.

17. Turn the notebook right side out and iron it. Edge stitch the opening closed.

18. Attach the leather button strap. Now you have a notebook to take with you on your travels.

Gold Clasped Makeup Bag

The finished makeup bag measures 6" x 4½" x 4¾" (15 x 11 x 12cm).

BEFORE YOU BEGIN:

- Use ⅜" (1cm) seam allowances unless indicated otherwise.

- Note that you'll need to refer to Essential Techniques A: Version 2 (p. 107). Note how the bottom lining requires a ¼" (0.5cm) seam allowance along the top edge.

- Find and trace the 3 pattern pieces from Side A of the pattern paper, remembering to add ⅜" (1cm) seam allowances.

- Be sure that when applying the ultra-firm interfacing to the main fabric, all the angles are perfectly straight.

CUT THE FOLLOWING PIECES FROM YOUR FABRIC AND INTERFACING:

Note that the interfacing for the bag body and sides is cut without seam allowances to reduce bulk.

- **Bag Flap:**
    - Top Layer (from pattern pack): Main outer fabric (1), Lining fabric (1), Heavyweight interfacing (1)
    - Bottom Layer (from pattern pack): Contrast fabric (2), Lining fabric (1), Heavyweight interfacing (2)

- **Bag Body** – cut a 6¾" x 11⅞" (17 x 30cm) rectangle: Main outer fabric (1), Lining fabric (1), Heavyweight interfacing (1), Ultra-firm interfacing (1)

- **Bag Sides** (from pattern pack): Main outer fabric (2), Lining fabric (2), Heavyweight interfacing (4)

- **Outside Pockets** – cut a 6¾" x 8" (17 x 20cm) rectangle: Main outer fabric (2), Heavyweight interfacing (2)

- **Inner Elastic Pocket** – cut an 8¼" x 8" (21 x 20cm) rectangle: Lining fabric (1), Heavyweight interfacing (1)

- **Inner Flat Pocket** – cut a 6¾" x 8" (17 x 20cm) rectangle: Lining fabric (1), Heavyweight interfacing (1)

MATERIALS:

- ⅓ yd. (⅓m) of medium-weight cotton fabric for outer bag

- ⅛ yd. (⅛m) of complementing light to medium-weight fabric for bag flap

- ⅓ yd. (⅓m) of lightweight cotton fabric for lining

- ⅓ yd. (⅓m) of 44" (112cm) wide or ⅔ yd. (⅔m) of 22" (56cm) wide heavyweight interfacing

- 6⅝" x 11⅞" (17 x 30cm) piece of ultra-firm fusible interfacing

- One 6" (15cm) gold purse frame

- About 15" (20cm) of flower border lace

- About 8" (20cm) of decorative lace

- One small (about 1½" [4cm]) decorative lace medallion

- At least 4½" (11cm) of ¼" (5.5mm) wide elastic

- ½" (1.5cm) sew-in snap

01. To make the front flap, see Essential Techniques A: Version 2 (p. 107). From the back of the flap, measure up 1" (2.5cm) from the bottom point and sew the prong side of the snap.

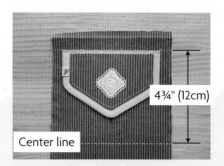

4¾" (12cm)

Center line

02. Cut down your heavyweight interfacing for the outer bag body to 6" x 11" (15 x 28cm). Center it onto the back of the corresponding outer bag fabric and iron it in place, making sure the edges are perfectly straight. Measure the bag body piece to find the center and mark a line horizontally across. Measure up 4¾" (12cm) from that center line and align the top of your front flap there. Sew it in place ¼" (0.5cm) down from the raw edge.

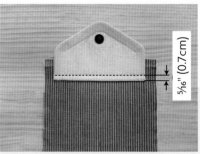

⁵⁄₁₆" (0.7cm)

03. Lift up the flap and sew ⁵⁄₁₆" (0.7cm) up from the previous seam, just enough to cover the raw edges from the previous seam. This completes the front flap of the bag.

04. Cut down your heavyweight interfacing for the outside pocket to 6" x 3½" (15 x 9cm). Center it towards the bottom of a corresponding outer bag fabric piece and iron it in place from the wrong side as the picture indicates. Your snap will be sewn here too, so you can apply another swatch of interfacing for strength. Sew the flower border lace on the edge of the other outer pocket.

05. Fold the pocket in half widthwise with right sides together. Sew a seam along the top raw edge and iron it.

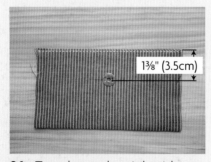

1⅜" (3.5cm)

06. Turn the pocket right side out so the outside shows. Edge stitch along the top edge. Sew the socket end of your snap 1⅜" (3.5cm) down from the top edge, and you've finished the front pocket!

07. To make the back pocket, follow steps 4-6 as for the front pocket. Sew an edge stitch along the top edge and the back pocket is finished!

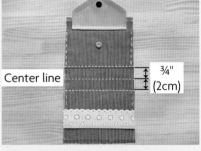

Center line

¾" (2cm)

08. Measure ¾" (2cm) up and down from the center line that was marked previously on the outer bag body piece. Align the bottom edges of the front pocket ¾" (2cm) up from the center (beneath the flap) and the back pocket ¾" (2cm) down from the center. Sew them in place along these bottom edges, and then fix the sides of the pocket in place with basting stitches.

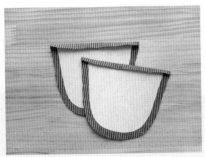

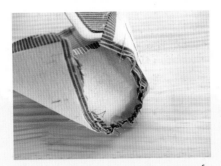

09. Iron the heavyweight interfacing bag side pieces onto their corresponding outer bag fabric pieces. Using the regular seam allowance, sew along the top edge of each piece, then fold down the edges along the seam line, ironing the fold in place.

10. Line up the bottom center of the bag side with the center line of your bag body piece. Line up the edges on each side, curving the bag body around the bag side, and sew the edges together. Repeat this with the other side of the bag.

11. Fold the seam allowances from the previous side seams toward the bag body. Fold under the top edges by ⅜" (1cm) and iron them in place, so the outside of your bag looks completely finished. Now you have finished the outside of the bag!

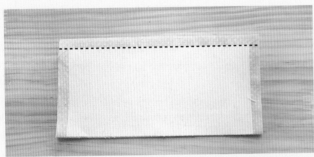

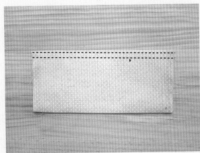

12. Cut down the interfacing pieces for your lining pockets to 7½" x 3½" (19 x 9cm) (elastic pocket) and 6" x 3½" (15 x 9cm) (flat-style). Iron the interfacing to their corresponding fabric pieces, centered along the bottom half of the pocket as in step 4. Apply the decorative lace to the flat pocket also as in step 4. Fold the pockets in half lengthwise so the top and bottom edges meet. Sew these edges together, then iron them.

13. Now turn both pockets right side out so that the correct side of the fabric is facing outwards. For the elastic pocket, sew two seams along the top to make the casing for the elastic. Sew one seam ⅛" (0.2cm) down from the top edge, and the other ⅜" (1cm) down from the top.

14. Use a bodkin to help work the elastic into the casing at the top of the pocket. Sew the elastic in place at each end when 4½" (11cm) of elastic is inside the casing, and trim the excess.

15. To make pleats at the bottom of the bag, find the center point along the bottom edge. Measure out 1⅝" (4cm) from the center and make a mark, then measure 2⅜" (6cm) and make another. Measure out from the other side of the center point by the same amounts to create four marks total. Fold the 1⅝" (4cm) points onto the 2⅜" (6cm) points to finish the pleats. Even out the folds, and baste them in place along the bottom edge.

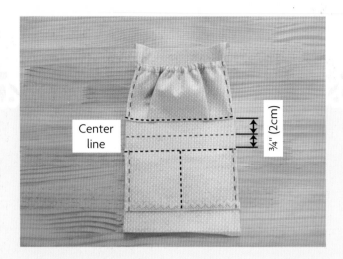

Center line

¾" (2cm)

16. Cut down the heavyweight interfacing for the Bag Body to 6" x 11" (15 x 28cm), and center it on the corresponding Bag Body Lining piece similar to step 2. Iron it in place with the edges perfectly straight. Measure the lining piece to find the center and mark a line horizontally across. Measure ¾" (2cm) up and down from this center line. Align the bottom edges of the inner pockets ¾" (2cm) and down from the center. Sew them in place along these bottom edges, and then fix the sides of the pocket in place with basting stitches.

17. Refer back to steps 9-11 to prepare your side lining pieces with interfacing and sew the lining pieces the same as the outer bag pieces for the sides of the bag. Once again, fold under the top edges so the top looks finished.

18. Nestle the lining into the main bag with the back sides of the lining and outer bag facing each other. Tack the lining in place from the inside to keep it from shifting. Line up the top folded edges.

19. Sew an edge stitch around the top outer edge of the bag.

20. Turn the bag inside out, and grab the center of the two sides of the bag, folding them in half, and sew a short tack ¼" (0.5cm) in from each fold.

21. Turn the bag right side out, and fit the gold purse frame evenly along the top of the bag. Fasten the frame to the bag. You have finished your stylish makeup bag!

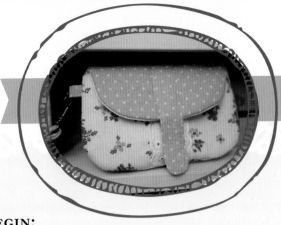

Handy Wristlet

The finished wristlet measures 6⅜" x 4" x ⅜" (16 x 10 x 1cm).

BEFORE YOU BEGIN:

- Use a ⅜" (1cm) seam allowance unless indicated otherwise.

- Find and trace the 3 pattern pieces from Side A of the pattern paper, remembering to add ⅜" (1cm) seam allowances.

CUT THE FOLLOWING PIECES FROM YOUR FABRIC AND INTERFACING:

Note that the heavyweight and fusible fleece interfacing is cut without seam allowances to reduce bulk.

- **Wristlet Flap Top** – cut a 7" x 4⅜" (18 x 11cm) rectangle: Contrast fabric – A (1)

- **Wristlet Flap Bottom** – cut a 7" x 3¾" (18 x 9.5cm) rectangle: Main outer fabric – B (1)

- **Wristlet Flap Lining** (from pattern pack): Lining fabric (1), Fusible fleece interfacing (1)

- **Wristlet Body** (from pattern pack): Main outer fabric – B (3), Lining fabric (3), Lightweight interfacing (3)

- **Zipper Pocket** – cut a 5⅞" x 5½" (15 x 14cm) rectangle: Lining fabric (1), Heavyweight interfacing (1)

- **Flap Tab** (from pattern pack): Contrast fabric – A (2), Heavyweight interfacing (1)

- **Wrist Strap** – cut a 1⅛" x 13¾" (3 x 35cm) rectangle: Contrast fabric – A (2), Heavyweight interfacing (1)

- **D-ring Loop** – cut a 1½" x 2" (4 x 5cm) rectangle: Contrast fabric – A (1)

MATERIALS:

- ¼ yd. (¼m) of light to medium-weight complementing fabric for flap, tab, and strap (Fabric A)

- ¼ yd. (¼m) of light to medium-weight fabric for main wristlet (Fabric B)

- ¼ yd. (¼m) of lightweight fabric for lining

- ¼ yd. (¼m) of lightweight interfacing

- ¼ yd. (¼m) of heavyweight interfacing

- 8" x 8" (20.5 x 20.5cm) fusible fleece interfacing

- 5" (12cm) zipper

- ⅜" (1cm) D-ring

- ⅜" (1cm) lobster clasp

- One metal rivet

- Magnetic snap

- 4¾" (12cm) of wide decorative lace

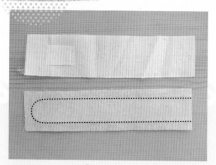

01. For the flap tab, iron on the interfacing. Layer the tab pieces together with right sides facing, then sew them together along the curved edge, leaving one straight edge free. Turn it right side out and iron it flat.

02. Line up the straight edges of the outer flap fabrics A and B with the tab sandwiched in between. Sew the layers together and press the seam allowance towards fabric B. When finished, use the wristlet flap lining pattern to trim the finished piece to the proper shape.

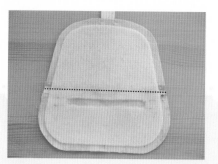

03. Take your fusible fleece interfacing and cut out the space for the zipper measuring 4" x ⅜" (10 x 1cm). Iron the fleece onto the wrong side of the outer flap fabric. On fabric B, edge stitch 1⁄16" (0.2cm) from the seam from the previous step.

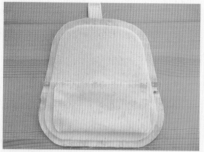

04. Iron the interfacing to the zipper pocket fabric, then use it to create a zipper pocket as seen in Essential Techniques F (p. 116).

05. Iron the rest of the interfacing pieces to their corresponding wristlet fabrics.

06. On one of the outer wristlet body pieces, sew a strip of decorative lace centered down the front of the fabric. Take the D-ring loop and fold the long edges under by ⅜" (1cm), then fold and sew the entire piece in half lengthwise with wrong sides together to create a strip. Sew the strip ¾" (2cm) down from the top edge of the fabric.

07. Take one of the outer wristlet body pieces and line it up with its corresponding lining piece with right sides together. Sew them along the top edge, trim the seam allowance, turn the fabric right side out, and press the seam. Repeat this with the other outer wristlet body and lining pieces twice more.

08. Apply the magnetic snap to the outer wristlet body fabric over the lace.

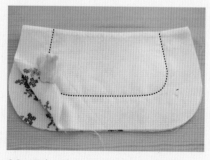

09. Take the remaining two wristlet body pieces and line them up with the outer sides facing. Sew them together along the stitching line indicated by the pattern.

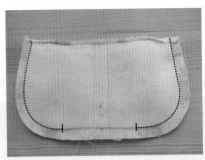

10. From the same piece, fold and pin back the top layers of the main and lining fabric towards the center against the seam from the previous step. This will reveal one layer each of outer and lining fabric along the bottom and side edges. Open up the last piece of outer fabric from step 6, and match up the side and bottom edges of the main fabric with that of the piece that has just been pinned back.

11. Sew the layers together along a 4" (10cm) section centered on the bottom edge.

12. Wrap the lining fabric around the wristlet to the other side, matching up the side and bottom edges. Sew it in place along the edges not covered by the previous step, skipping over the 4" (10cm) section in the bottom center.

13. Turn the wristlet right side out through the opening in the bottom, then edge stitch the opening closed. Loop the D-ring through the fabric strip at the corner of the wristlet body, then baste the other end of the strip to the corner of the remaining outer wristlet body piece ⅜" (1cm) down from the top edge.

14. Layer the wristlet flap fabric over the wristlet body fabric with right sides together. Tuck back the section with the lace, and focus on matching the edges of the remaining wristlet body fabric. Sew these layers together with a 4" (10cm) long seam centered along the bottom edge.

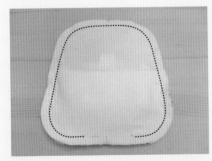

15. Iron the interfacing to the flap lining, then layer it beneath the fabric just sewn with right sides facing and match up the raw edges. Sew it in place by covering the area not sewn in the previous step, skipping over the 4" (10cm) section at the bottom.

16. Trim the seam allowances and turn the wristlet right side out, then sew the opening closed. Edge stitch the flap tab to secure it in place, then attach the magnetic snap.

17. See Essential Techniques H (p. 119) to learn how to create the strap, and attach it to your D-ring. Your handy wristlet is now finished!

Essential Techniques

A Quick Guide to Useful Sewing Tricks

A. Three-Dimensional Bag Flaps

B. Flat Bag Flaps

C. Compartment Pockets

D. Three-Dimensional Pockets

E. Elastic Pockets

F. Zipper Pockets

G. Purse Feet

H. Wrist Straps

I. Shoulder Straps

J. Leather-Bordered Labels

K. Bias Binding

L. Piping

M. Magnetic Snaps and Push-Lock Clasps

BEFORE YOU BEGIN:

- If you use a fabric like cotton burlap, only a single layer of interfacing is needed for the outer fabric, as any more would create too much bulk.

- If you attach a push-lock style clasp to the flap, you'll need to apply an extra layer of interfacing to the lining fabric to reinforce it. Attach the clasp before sewing the flap to the bag body.

Version 1: Single Layer Flap: 2 pieces of fabric (outer fabric and lining)

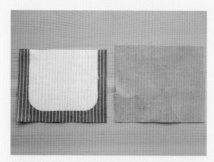

01. When cutting the flap pieces, it is not necessary to add a seam allowance to the top edge of the outer fabric. Add a ¼" (0.5cm) seam allowance to the top edge of the lining fabric. You can roughly cut the fabric first, iron the interfacing, sew the seam, and then trim it afterwards.

02. Place the outer fabric and lining pieces together with right sides facing. Sew a seam along the side and bottom edges to anchor them in place. Trim the seam allowances along the rounded edges.

03. Turn the flap right side out and iron it. Edge stitch around the side and bottom edges to secure the edges together. You'll see that the lining fabric extends slightly beyond the outer fabric.

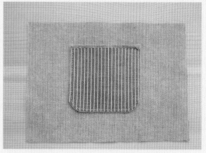

04. Place the flap on the main fabric of the bag with the right sides both facing up. Sew a seam just outside the edge of the outer fabric.

05. Lift the flap up and with a seam allowance of 5/16" (0.7cm), sew a seam to secure the flap.

06. You have finished your bag flap.

Version 2: Double-Layered Flap: 4 pieces of fabric (outer fabric and lining for the top layer, outer fabric and lining for the bottom layer)

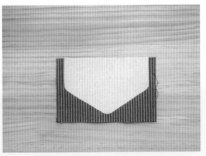

01. Align the interfacing on the top edge of the outer fabric top layer. The outer fabric does not need a seam allowance for the top edge.

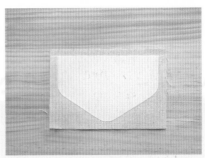

02. On the top edge of the lining fabric for the bottom layer, leave a ¼" (0.5cm) seam allowance.

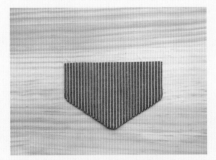

03. Place the top layer fabrics together with right sides facing and sew a seam around the edges. Clip the seam allowances with pinking shears and turn the fabric right side out. Apply the lace medallion called for in your pattern if applicable.

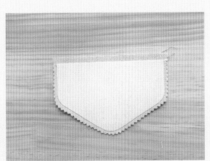

04. Follow the same instructions for the bottom layer fabric pieces.

05. Line up the top layer over the bottom layer of fabric (tuck the monogrammed ribbon in between if your project includes it) and edge stitch around the top layer to join them together. Attach the magnetic button if applicable.

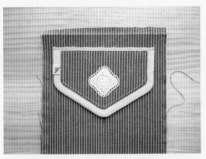

06. Line up the flap on the main body of the bag and sew a seam just outside the outer fabric to join the fabric together.

07. Lift up the flap and sew a seam with a ⁵⁄₁₆" (0.7cm) seam allowance.

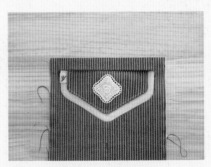

08. Your flap is complete!

Version 1: Single Layer Flap: 2 pieces of fabric (outer fabric and lining)

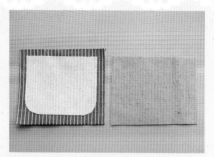

01. When applying the interfacing, note that the outer fabric should have a ¼" (0.5cm) seam allowance along the top edge, while the lining fabric needs no seam allowance along the top edge.

02. Layer the outer fabric and lining together with right sides facing and sew them together along the side and bottom edges.

03. Trim the edges with pinking shears, this will make the shape of the flap look better.

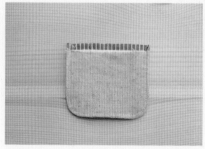

04. Turn the flap right side out and iron it. Edge stitch around the edges to secure it. Note how the outer fabric extends beyond the lining.

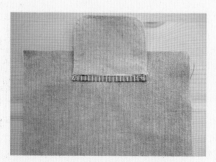

05. Place the flap on the main fabric of the bag with right sides facing each other. Sew a seam just outside the edge of the lining fabric.

06. Fold the flap bag down, and sew another seam 5⁄16" (0.7cm) down from the folded edge to finish the flap.

Version 2: Double-Layered Flap: A total of four pieces of fabric (top layer outer fabric and lining, bottom layer outer fabric and lining)

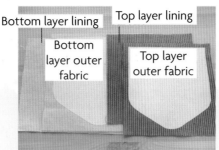

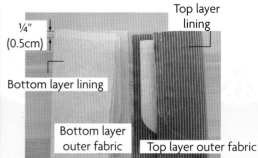

01. Iron the interfacing to the fabric pieces. The top layer outer fabric, lining, and bottom layer outer fabric need a ¼" (0.5cm) seam allowance along the top edge.

02. Line up the top layer outer fabric and lining together with right sides facing and sew a seam around the side and bottom edges to join them. Repeat this with the bottom layers of fabric.

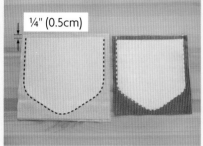

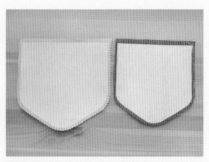

03. Note how the outer fabric of the bottom layer extends beyond the lining.

04. Trim the seam allowances with pinking shears.

05. Turn the fabric right side out and iron it. Apply the decorative lace medallion to the top layer (if the project includes it) and edge stitch along the edges of the bottom layer of fabric.

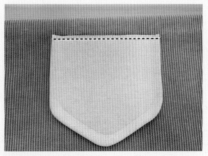

06. Align the top layer onto the bottom layer (tuck the monogrammed ribbon in between if your project includes it) and edge stitch the top layer in place. Attach the magnetic snap to the flap.

07. Place the flap on the main fabric with right sides facing and sew a seam on the edge of the interfacing, just outside the lining fabric.

08. Lift up the flap and sew it in place ⁵⁄₁₆" (0.7cm) from the folded edge to finish the flap.

Version 1: Total of One Piece of Fabric: inner and outer fabric as the same piece

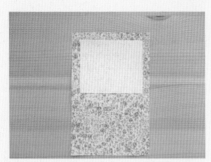

01. Iron the interfacing onto what will be the outside of the pocket. The interfacing does not require a seam allowance.

02. Fold the fabric in half with right sides facing so the bottom edge meets the top edge. Sew a seam along the sides, leaving a small opening at the top.

03. Iron the seam and trim the four corners, being sure not to cut the bottom.

04. Turn the fabric right side out and iron it. Sew a seam along the top edge of the pocket.

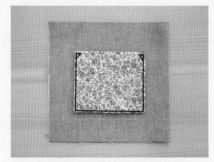

05. Align the pocket wherever you would like to place it, and sew a seam around the sides and bottom to set it in place. On the top two edges you can sew a triangle-shaped seam to make the pocket more secure.

Version 2: Total of Two Pieces of Fabric: separate fabrics for the outside and inner pocket

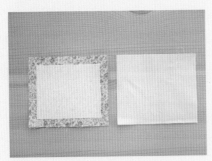

01. Iron the interfacing to the fabric that will be the outer pocket, positioning it in the center. Make sure to leave seam allowances on all four sides of the fabric.

02. Place the outer pocket and pocket lining fabrics together with front sides facing. Sew a seam along all the edges, leaving a small opening in one side.

03. Iron the seam and trim the four corners, making sure not to cut the seams.

04. Turn the fabric right side out and iron it. Sew a seam along the top edge.

05. Line up the pocket on the main fabric and sew a seam around the side and bottom edges.

Version 3: Pocket sewn directly onto the main fabric of the bag

01. Iron the interfacing onto what will be the outside pocket. Place the interfacing aligned with the center of the fabric.

02. Fold down the top edge of the fabric to meet the bottom edge with wrong sides together and iron it. Edge stitch along the fold.

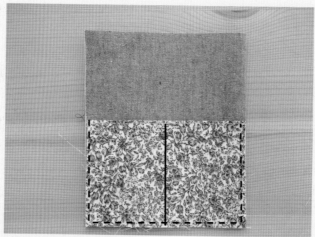

03. Line up the pocket on the bag's main fabric and baste it in place along the bottom and side edges. If needed, you can also sew a seam down the center of the pocket in order to create separate compartments.

D: Three-Dimensional Pockets

Version 1: Sewn onto the center of the main body of the bag

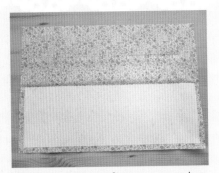

01. Iron the interfacing onto what will be the outer pocket fabric. Line up the interfacing along the center line.

02. Fold down the top edge to meet the bottom edge with right sides together and sew a seam along the side and bottom edges. Be sure to leave an opening along the bottom edge.

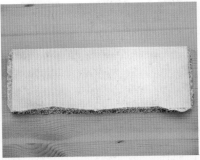

03. Trim the four corners and iron the seam.

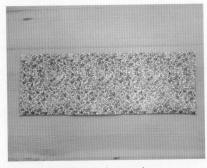

04. Turn the pocket right side out and iron it. Make the marks required by the project directions or according to your specific needs.

05. Along each fold line, sew a pin tuck.

06. The finished pocket will resemble a ⊓ shape.

07. Layer the finished pocket over the main fabric of the bag, folding together the pin tucks to create the inverted pleats that will be your three-dimensional sections. Sew the pocket in place along the sides and bottom edges as well as the marked separation lines.

08. You have completed your three-dimensional pocket.

Version 2: Sewn directly onto the main fabric of the bag

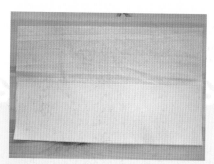

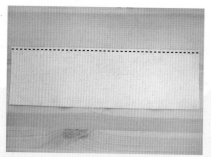

01. First iron the interfacing onto what will be the outer pocket fabric. Align the interfacing along the center folding line.

02. Fold the top edge down to meet the bottom edge and iron the fabric. Edge stitch along the top edge of the fold to secure it.

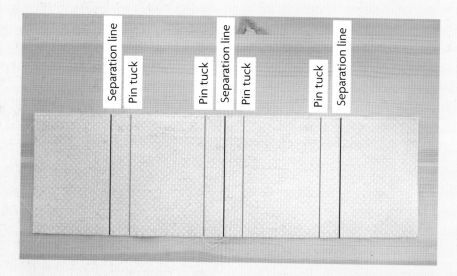

03. According to the project instructions, mark the placement of the pin tuck lines and separation lines.

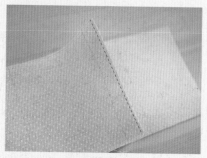

04. Fold the fabric up along these pin tuck lines and sew a pin tuck there.

05. The finished pocket will resemble a Π shape.

06. Lay the pocket onto the main fabric of the bag and fold the pin tucks in place to create the three-dimensional sections. Sew seams along the sides and bottom as well as the separation lines to finish your pocket.

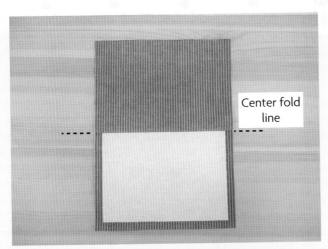

01. First iron the interfacing onto what will be the outer pocket fabric, making sure to line up the interfacing along the center fold line of the fabric.

02. Fold the top edge of the fabric towards the bottom edge and iron it flat. Sew two seams along the top edge of the fabric, first an edge stitch close to the fold, then another seam ⅜" (1cm) from the previous seam. The width here depends on the width of the elastic you choose.

03. Thread the elastic through the channel you've just sewn, then baste the elastic ends in place as it is guided through.

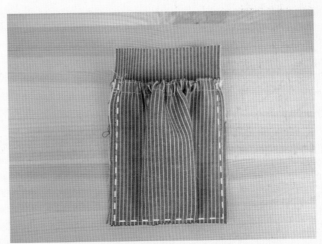

04. Align the pocket onto the main fabric for the bag, make any pleats in the pocket as the project requires, and baste it in place along the side and bottom edges.

 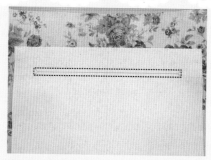

01. Iron the interfacing to the pocket fabric. Mark the placement lines for the zipper opening. Layer the pocket fabric over the main bag fabric with right sides facing and use pins to hold it in place.

02. Sew a seam around the rectangle that forms the zipper opening.

 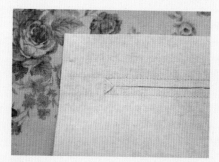

03. Use a seam ripper to start to open up the zipper opening.

04. Use scissors to cut open the rest of the opening, cutting along the marks as close as possible to the seam without cutting through it.

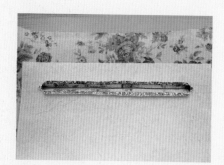 

05. Open up the small flaps you've just cut and iron them flat.

06. Feed the pocket fabric through the opening.

07. Turn the pocket fabric to the other side and iron it flat.

08. Use fusible web to anchor the zipper in place onto the back side of the fabric while you sew it. Edge stitch completely around the opening to anchor the zipper in place.

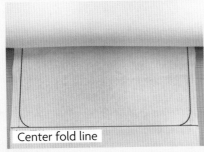

Center fold line

09. Fold the bottom edge of the pocket up to meet the top edge. Draw rounded corners along the bottom side seams.

10. Sew the edges of the pocket fabric together, lifting up the sides of the outer fabric if it gets in the way.

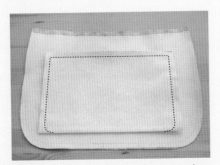

11. The sewn edges of the pocket fabric should resemble this.

12. You have now finished your zipper pocket.

01. Purse feet come in all different shapes and sizes, so choose your feet according to the measurements of the product that you are making in order to find feet which best suit your bag.

02. Make marks on your plastic board for where you will punch holes for your purse feet. Trim the four corners to make them rounded.

03. Pull your purse fabric around the plastic board and sew a gathering seam to gather the fabric around the edges of the board. Cover the board enough so the plastic won't damage the fabric of your bag.

04. Use a hole punch to make the openings for the purse feet.

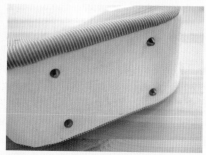

05. Punch holes in the main fabric of the bag. Attach the purse feet from the outside of the bag and pull the prongs through the plastic board.

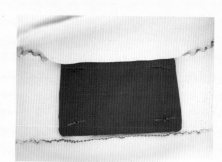

06. If the purse feet have spacers, then pull them through these spacers and then finish attaching them to your plastic board.

H: Wrist Straps

01. To make a ⅜" (1cm) wide strap, trim two pieces of 1⅛" (3cm) wide fabric, and iron a ⅜" (1cm) wide strip of interfacing onto the center.

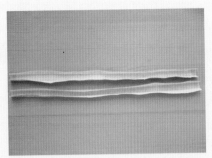

02. Fold under ⅜" (1cm) on each long side of the strap and iron the folds down.

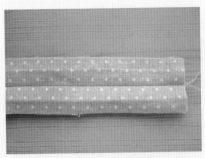

03. Layer the two pieces together with right sides facing, and sew them together along one long side. Open the fabric out and iron the seam.

04. Slide the D-ring onto the strap, then sew the two pieces together along each short end, creating a ring.

05. Fold the fabric back together so the right side is facing outward and iron the strap flat. Use strong clips to hold the folds together and fasten it in place.

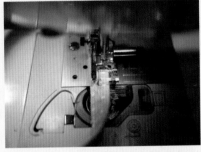

06. Edge stitch along each side to secure the strap.

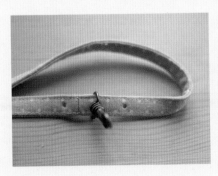

07. Punch two holes in the strap about 1½" (4cm) away from each other with the D-ring in the middle.

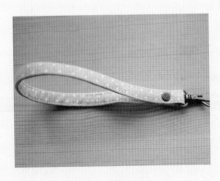

08. Attach a metal rivet here to finish your strap.

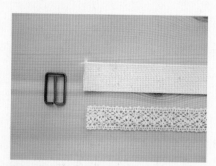

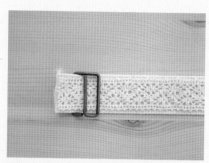

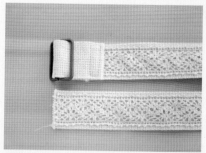

01. If you would like to use decorative lace in your strap, first sew it onto complementing webbing or similar strap material.

02. Slide the strap through the strap adjuster from the left side.

03. Loop the fabric through the adjuster, and fold under the edge twice. Sew the folds in place with a box stitch.

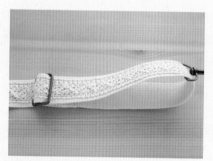

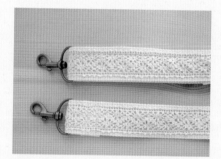

04. From the other end of the strap, slide on the hook ring, then loop the strap through the strap adjuster again.

05. With the remaining raw end, loop it through a second hook ring, then fold under the fabric twice and sew it in place with a box stitch.

01. Fold under the sides of the cotton label and iron it flat. Roughly cut a piece of leather larger than the cotton label.

02. Layer the cotton label over the leather and edge stitch it in place.

03. Trim the leather near the edges of the cotton fabric to finish your label.

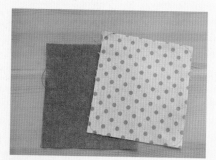

01. Prepare the outer fabric and lining.

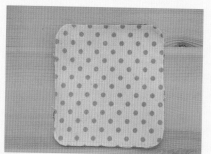

02. Layer them together with wrong sides facing and baste them together around the raw edges.

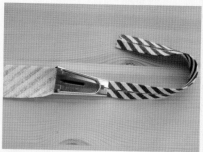

03. Use a bias tape maker to fold your bias strip of fabric. Iron the folds in place.

04. Line up one fold of the bias tape around the perimeter of your main fabric. Fold under the beginning edge of the tape by ⅜" (1cm), then sew it in place around the fabric, overlapping the ending edge of the tape over the beginning by ⅜" (1cm) when you make it all the way around.

05. Wrap the bias tape around the edge of the main fabric, bringing the second fold to the other side. Iron the fold in place, then sew around the edges once again to finish the border.

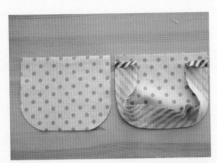

01. Take a strip of bias fabric and fold the two short edges under by ⅜" (1cm). Baste one long edge to your outer fabric.

02. Layer a piece of twine or cotton cord inside the bias strip, then wrap the fabric around the cording, folding it in half. Baste the fold in place along the edge of the main fabric.

03. Layer the lining fabric over the outer fabric and pin it in place, matching up the edges.

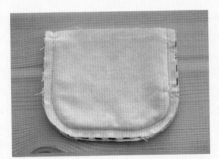

04. Sew the seam as before, using a zipper foot to sew as close as possible to the cording.

05. Trim the seam allowances at the corners and turn the fabric right side out. Your piping is now finished.

01. The application of magnetic snaps and push-locks should be the same and they should all have base backings.

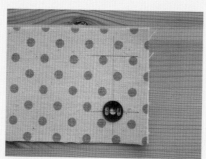

02. First determine in advance the placement of the snap by making crosshair marks on the fabric. Draw the placement mark for the base of the snap using the spacer.

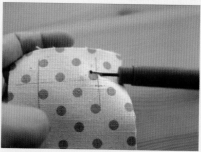

03. Use a seam ripper to cut an opening for the base.

04. Insert the base of the magnetic snap into the opening.

05. The snap should look like the picture when viewed from the back.

06. Attach the spacer onto the snap base, then bend the prongs evenly outward.

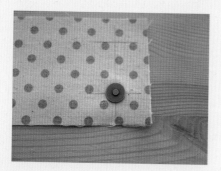

07. Now you have finished your magnetic snap.

Index

Note: Page numbers in *italics* indicate
projects

B
Backpack, *30–31, 77–81*
bag flaps
    flat, 108–9
    three-dimensional, 106–7
bags
    about: overview of projects, 10–11
    Backpack, *30–31, 77–81*
    Casual Day Trip Purse, *20–21,
      59–61*
    Drawstring Bucket Purse, *16–17,
      53–54*
    Evening Bag, *14–15, 50–52*
    Everything Bag, *24–25, 65–69*
    Lunch Bag, *22–23, 62–64*
    Travel Purse, *26–27, 70–74*
    Vintage Gold Clasped Purse, *28–29,
      75–76*
    Weekend Bag, *18–19, 55–58*
    Working Girl's Shoulder Bag,
      12–13, 46–49
bias binding, 122

C
Casual Day Trip Purse, *20–21, 59–61*
Chic Coin Purse, *36–37, 87–89*
clasps, push-lock, 124
Classy Clutch, *38–39, 90–92*
clutches and accessories
    about: overview of projects, 32–33
    Chic Coin Purse, *36–37, 87–89*
    Classy Clutch, *38–39, 90–92*
    Compartment Clutch, *34–35, 82–86*
    Gold Clasped Makeup Bag, *42–43,
      97–100*
    Handy Wristlet, *44, 101–3*
    Travel Notebook, *40–41, 93–96*
coin purse, *36–37, 87–89*
Compartment Clutch, *34–35, 82–86*
compartment pockets, 110–12

D
Drawstring Bucket Purse, *16–17,
53–54*

E
elastic pockets, 115
Evening Bag, *14–15, 50–52*
Everything Bag, *24–25, 65–69*

F
feet, purse, 118
flat bag flaps, 108–9

G
Gold Clasped Makeup Bag, *42–43*

H
Handy Wristlet, *44, 101–3*

L
labels, leather-bordered, 121
Lunch Bag, *22–23, 62–64*

M
magnetic strips, 124
makeup bag, *42–43, 97–100*

N
notebook, travel, *40–41, 93–96*

P
piping, 123
pockets
    compartment, 110–12
    elastic, 115
    three-dimensional, 113–14
    zipper, 116–17
purse feet, 118
purses. *See* bags
push-lock clasps, 124

S
sewing techniques
    bias binding, 122
    compartment pockets, 110–12
    elastic pockets, 115
    flat bag flaps, 108–9
    leather-bordered labels, 121
    magnetic strips and push-lock
      clasps, 124
    piping, 123
    purse feet, 118
    shoulder straps, 120
    three-dimensional bag flaps, 106–7
    three-dimensional pockets, 113–14
    wrist straps, 119
    zipper pockets, 116–17
shoulder straps, 120
straps
    shoulder, 120
    wrist, 119

T
three-dimensional bag flaps, 106–7
three-dimensional pockets, 113–14
Travel Notebook, *40–41, 93–96*
Travel Purse, *26–27, 70–74*

V
Vintage Gold Clasped Purse, *28–29,
75–76*

W
Weekend Bag, *18–19, 55–58*
Working Girl's Shoulder Bag, *12–13,
46–49*
wrist straps, 119
wristlet, *44, 101–3*

Z
zipper pockets, 116–17

More Pretty Little Things from Cherie Lee

If you love the simple elegance of *Sewing Pretty Little Things,* you'll be glad to hear there's more to come! Cherie Lee's next book from Design Originals will offer even more exquisite accessories for you to sew, using just fabric remnants and little scraps of cloth.

Cherie will show you how to give new purpose to special pieces of material, by transforming them into a variety of wonderful accessories—from sun hats and slippers to camera bags, coin purses, mobile phone cases, and much more. You'll discover imaginative ideas for making useful items and meaningful gifts featuring her classic, beautiful designs.

ISBN 978-1-57421-861-9 **$19.99**
DO5435

Look for Cherie Lee's upcoming sequel at your local bookstore or specialty retailer, or at d-originals.com

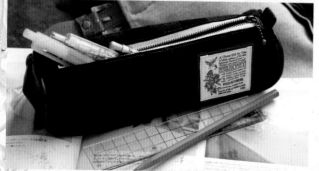

More Great Books from Design Originals

**Handmade Leather
Bags & Accessories**
ISBN 978-1-57421-716-2 **$19.99**
DO5036

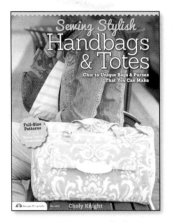

**Sewing Stylish
Handbags & Totes**
ISBN 978-1-57421-422-2 **$22.99**
DO5393

Sew Me! Sewing Basics
ISBN 978-1-57421-423-9 **$19.99**
DO5394

Sew Me! Sewing Home Décor
ISBN 978-1-57421-504-5 **$14.99**
DO5425

Sewing Leather Accessories
ISBN 978-1-57421-623-3 **$14.99**
DO5313

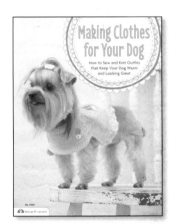

Making Clothes for Your Dog
ISBN 978-1-57421-610-3 **$19.99**
DO5300

Sew Fun for Girls & Dolls
ISBN 978-1-57421-364-5 **$11.99**
DO3487

Seaside Quilts
ISBN 978-1-57421-431-4 **$24.99**
DO5402

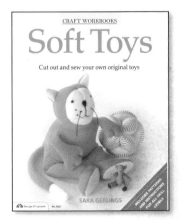

Soft Toys
ISBN 978-1-57421-501-4 **$9.99**
DO5422